ACTING IS STORYTELLING

ACTING
IS
STORYTELLING©

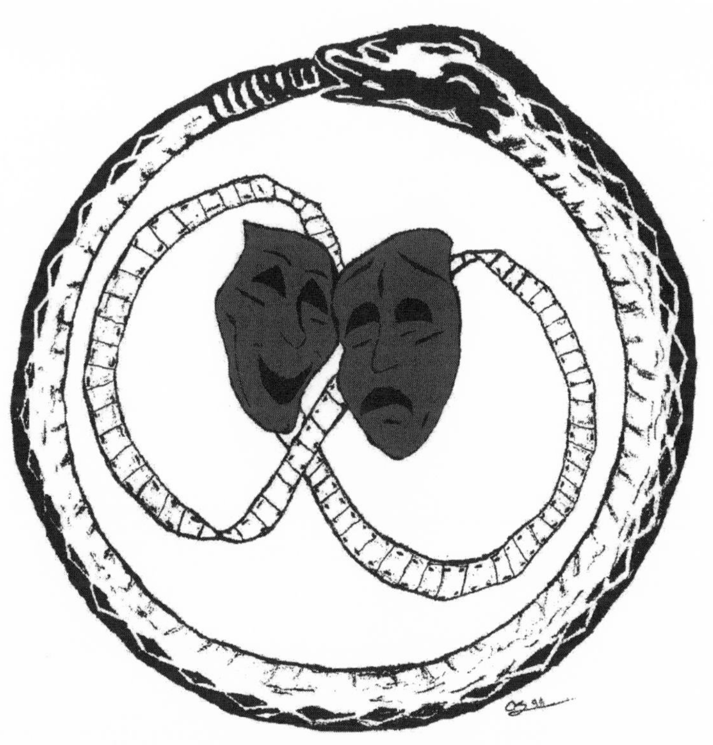

ACTING IS STORYTELLING

BY

KEN FARMER

Edited and with an Introduction by

PETER BROWN

DEDICATED TO:

This book is dedicated to all actors who are committed and have a never-ending desire to learn: to my good friend, Peter Brown, for his support, suggestions and proofreading of this book and to Gene Hackman and Cliff Osmond, who taught me what *good* acting was really all about.

GOOD ACTING IS NEVER OBSERVED;
IT IS EXPERIENCED.

My apologies to anyone I may have offended by the use of the "masculine" throughout this book. Since we are "all" now referred to as *Actors,* it was easier and saved space by using he or his instead of he/she or his/her. - KEN FARMER

ISBN: 978-0-9848820-2-1

Published by:
Timber Creek Press
Published in the USA

6308 West Line Rd. Gainesville, Texas 76240 - Cell - 214-533-4964
pagact@yahoo.com www.kenfarmer.mysite.com

TIMBER CREEK PRESS

INTRODUCTION
by PETER BROWN

I have never written an introduction for a book of any kind before,... but I have read and studied many, many books on the art and craft of acting. I have had the privilege and good fortune of being taught by some of the finest teachers and coaches in the business.

First, by my mother, *Mina Reaume,* who was both a stage and radio actress in New York; then from *Dr. Ralph Freud*, head of the drama department at UCLA. I later studied under *Jeff Corey*, with classmates, among others, *Jack Nicholson, Martin Landau* and *Sally Kellerman*. Finally, I learned a great deal from *John Russell*, my costar on the *"Lawman"* television series. John was a very serious and well-trained actor as well as my friend and mentor.

However, my greatest teacher thus far has been experience. The first time a young actor discovers that the instrument he is walking around in is actually *trainable* to do and express exactly the aspects and personality of any character the individual can dream up, and the response to any given situation within the context of a scene comes from the *preparation* of the *"BACKSTORY"*, is simply amazing. I have long had the reputation for having a photographic mind when it comes to learning lines. I didn't know it at the time, but I have been using The PAG System all these years intuitively.

Before I go any further, let me fill the reader in on some of the background between Ken Farmer and Peter Brown... I don't exactly remember where and when we actually met, but it seems like I've known Ken since I was a kid actor growing up on the Warner Brother's lot; lucky enough (if you believe in luck) to be learning my film acting craft by doing it. We would shoot almost every single day... making 39 episodes a season. Add to that 13 reruns in the summer and you had your 52 weeks for the year.

When we did have a hiatus (a fancy word for a break) they would send me to Manila or some other Godforsaken place, dress me up like a soldier and send me out to act in the swamps. I loved it..., every minute..., well, maybe not every minute... but I did love it.

To get back to Ken;... one of those "Most Unforgettable Characters I've ever met". Ken is cowboy... in the best sense of the word. Ken is one of the most genuine, honorable men I've ever had the good fortune to call my friend, and he is that because of who and what he is. There's no middle ground with Ken; like every stunt man I've ever known... you're his friend or you're not. You're in his life or you're not, you always know where you stand. I don't think he could even define wishy-washy if you asked him to, but he could, and would, give you his opinion on just about any topic you'd choose to come up with; even at the risk of losing, whether it be a job or a relationship, either personal or professional. If you don't want an *honest* answer, go somewhere else... don't ask Ken Farmer.

Add to that the fact that he's the best damn hand at a barbecue you can imagine. I would share his campfire anytime. He'd also be the one I would choose to watch my back in any circumstance, matter of fact, I wouldn't have to choose him, he'd be there, and has been, without asking.

Enough with the character reference...Ken had asked me if I would proof, edit and write the introduction for this book; in doing so, I put his well-defined system of learning the words to the test. So help me, it works...you don't really have to concern yourself with the words once you know and focus on the story completely.

In short, this is the finest, easiest to understand handbook and guide for the New Age Actor, (or any actor of any age, for that matter) that I have ever come across. In the first reading of this, I would suggest you set aside a couple of hours to read it cover to cover, taking your good sweet time in doing so. Not a bad idea to gather a few of your friends together (I know they're actors, too) and read it aloud together and try some of the material out and critique it. Acting is sharing; so why not also share the learning experience?

Ken is one of the best teachers/coaches I have had the good fortune to personally watch work with his students, first hand.... treat yourself to this book, you'll be grateful your entire career. It will become your acting Bible.

Break-a-leg! - Peter Brown

ABOUT THE AUTHOR

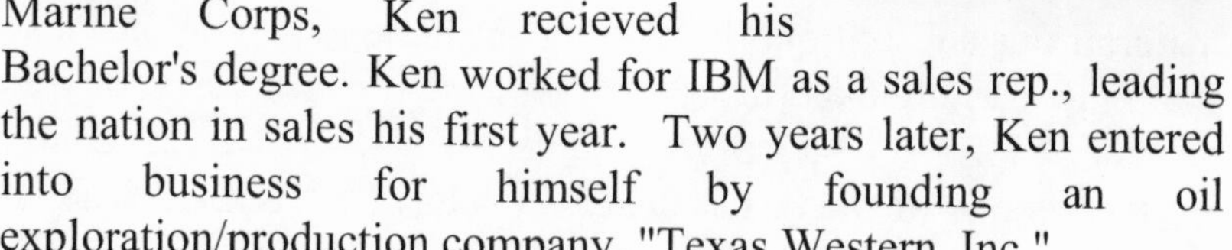

Ken Farmer was born in the small East Texas oil boomtown of Kilgore. The son of a Texas wildcatter, Ken attended over 21 grade schools in 7 states, living in almost every boomtown of the time.

After graduating from Gainesville, Texas, (high school). Ken attended Oklahoma University, then Stephen F. Austin State University on full football scholarship. Majoring in Business and Speech & Drama, after a stint in the Marine Corps, Ken recieved his Bachelor's degree. Ken worked for IBM as a sales rep., leading the nation in sales his first year. Two years later, Ken entered into business for himself by founding an oil exploration/production company, "Texas Western, Inc.".

It was during the period he was CEO of Texas Western, that Ken became interested in professional acting, having heretofore relegated his drama training to "Little Theater, Community Playhouse, etc.". He was talked into auditioning for a Dairy Queen commercial by Dallas agent, Kim Dawson. They needed a real cowboy and Ken also owned a working cattle ranch in East Texas where he raised registered Beefmaster cattle and Quarter Horses. Suffice to say, Ken got the part. (That's another story.) That was over two hundred sixty commercials (some of which he Produced and Directed), twelve major feature films and over fifty TV shows and TV movies ago and only God knows how many Industrials. Ken was the television spokesman for Wolf Brand Chili for eight years and most recently appeared in “FRIDAY NIGHT LIGHTS”, “THE NEWTON BOYS”, “ROCKETMAN”, “LOGAN’S WAR”, “THE PRESIDENT’S MAN”, six episodes of “WALKER, TEXAS RANGER” and

“THE GOOD GUYS”. Ken has worked with many award winning actors; Billy Bob Thornton, Gene Hackman, Lucus Black, Robert Stack, Linda Hunt, Kevin Kline, Kevin Costner, Peter Fonda, James Woods, Peter Brown, Brian Dennehy, Howard Keel, Jeff Goldblum, Elizabeth Ashley, Karen Allen, Danny Glover, Kris Kristofferson, Rip Torn, Robert Fuller, Slim Pickens, Robert Conrad, Scott Glenn, Bo Bridges, Larry Hagman, Willie Nelson, Ethan Hawk, Matthew McConaughey and John Cleese, to name a few. Ken has been known to say, "I can't believe they actually want to pay me for something I love to do so much, I guess my avocation has become my vocation."

In 1984, Ken had a major role in "SILVERADO" and decided to devote full time to acting and moved to Los Angles. While in L. A., Ken continued his acting studies at the Actor's Center.

Ken has also written several projects in addition to this book, including the screen plays, "SLEEPING DOG", an action adventure-romantic-comedy set in Texas, “ROCKABILLY BABY”, a 50’s era rock and roll drama and “BONE!” a cop who-done-it sci/fy dramady MOW/Pilot. Additionally, Ken and his partner, Buck Stienke founded Timber Creek Productions, LLC, specifically to acquire and produce quality film projects. Some of the acquisitions include "THE TUMBLEWEED WAGON" (which Ken has done several major rewrites on), "THE PEACE OFFICER", “BONE”, "SLEEPING DOG", "BAD MOON RISING", and “ROCKABILLY BABY”. Timber Creek Productions completed post production of “ROCKABILLY BABY” June 12, 2008. Ken wrote and directed the feature, starring Denton Blane Everett, Todd Farr and Brandi Price.

Ken and his writing partner, Buck Stienke, recently released their first novel, *BLACK EAGLE FORCE: Eye of the Storm*. www.blackeagleforce.com. The second novel, *BLACK EAGLE FORCE: Sacred Mountain*, is now complete as is the third, *RETURN of the STARFIGHTER* and fourth, *THE NATIONS*, a historical fiction action western. All four published by Timber Creek Press and are available on Amazon, Barnes & Noble and wherever good books are sold in paper or E versions. All of the Black Eagle Force novels are in Amazon's Best Seller top 100 list. We are almost complete with number five, *BLACK EAGLE FORCE: Blood Ivory* and Ken has started one on his own, another historical fiction western with a supernatural twist; *THE FALLS.*

In addition to an active acting and writing career, Ken started coaching acting fourteen years ago. It was during one of his workshops, that someone asked why he didn't write a book on the style of acting he was teaching (Storytelling) because it was so logical and easy to understand and it would give the students a text to study outside of class. (nuff said,... here 'tis).

Ken currently lives in rural North Texas (with his five dogs and two cats near Gainesville. Ken is married to Kat Steele, has one son, Clay and two grand daughters, Makena and Morgan, currently residing in Houston, Texas. Ken is also a lifetime member of the alumni association of Stephen F. Austin State University as well as a lifetime member of the "T" association (letterman's club).

Forward

FROM THE DESK OF ALEX CORD

Alex Cord, star of over 41 features and innumerable TV shows, including "ARCHANGEL" in the series, "*AIRWOLF*", recently sent me this letter after reading a draft of this book:

Dear Kenny,

I think you've done a superb job! Taking out the mystique and getting down to what it's really all about; telling the story through hard work and a creative imagination. Great exercises. I particularly liked the idea that the other guy's words are as important as your own and highlighting the power words in everyone's dialogue. It's very impressive work. I truly wish you every success. You deserve it.

I see far too much abominable posing trying to pass as acting. Every aspiring actor should be obliged to learn your book from cover to cover before ever attempting to develop a character. Perhaps then we would be spared some of the torturous performances we've all had to endure.

Good luck and God bless. Thank you very much for sharing your wisdom with me. I feel honored..
Your friend,
Alex Cord

MORE COMMENTS

Ken,

I know you haven't heard from me in a long time, but I have been thinking about 'you' a lot! I take your book to most all of my auditions. I tell everyone that I meet (actors mostly) about this wonderful book ("ACTING IS STORYTELLING) that you have written. I am still very interested in taking your class on a regular basis. I am just trying to work it out.

I have read more acting books and been to more coaches, classes, and seminars, from NY to LA and places in between, than I care to mention.

In all of that I have never read a more insightful, exciting, common sense approach to acting. And It Works! I haven't booked every job that I have auditioned for since I read "ACTING IS STORYTELLING", but what has happened is now when I prepare for an audition, no matter how silly, dramatic, large or small, I now have a sure fire way of preparing, learning, or in some cases creating the story. I go in with a new kind of confidence and I find that my gift is always available to me now. I just had to let you know this...

I only wish I had read your book before I booked my second episode of 'Walker'. I didn't do a terrible job or anything but in a couple of places 'I' can see the 'wheels'. In other places 'I' can't see the wheels and it appears to be seamless but the emotional price I paid to get there was 'huge'.

Thank you for taking the time to write this book. - ***Silvia Mathis Moore*** **- Actress**

Ken,

I came to your class with the expressed need to increase my "memorization of lines" skills. In short order, I learned from you and through your book, that memorization is the very bane of the actor's skills. In short order, I learned from you that I embarrassingly missed the point of this craft: Storytelling. When I learned about the story, and how to tell the story from different perspectives, I confess, I did not think this was going to help my poor retention skills. I was profoundly surprised by the first class that after doing the exercise you prescribed, how quickly and deeply ingrained the words naturally came---once the story was learned ! I use this prescribed technique now and will not do without it in my "tool chest". Thank you for the shock. I needed a wake up call. I was sleepier than I thought.

My sincere thanks,- ***B. Kaarina Turning*** **- Actress**

MIKE MOROFF Jan. 14, 2006

Actor/Singer,- Select movies- "Desperado", "Night of The Living Dead III", "Scarface", "Rambo III", "Born in East L.A.", "Shoot to Kill", "La Bamba", "RoboCop". TV - Air America, The Magnificent Seven, The Sentinel, Adventures of Young Indiana Jones and many more.

My Amigo, Ken,

I hope Santa brought you what you wanted this year and here is to working in the craft that we love the most in 2006.

All I can say about your book is "Oh my God! Brilliant!" The only thing that I didn't like about your book is that it wasn't around when I started my acting career. As you know, some of us cannot afford to go to acting schools, acting workshops, or even colleges and universities for drama. We have to learn while we earn.

"Acting is Storytelling" should be mandatory reading for anyone who wants to be an actor or any other position in the industry. You give people a great foundation to begin and further their career. The writing is so simple that it inspires. The basics are right there for even the earliest beginner to understand. Even someone like me, who comes from the "University of Hard Knocks", can learn so much from this book.

Ken, where were you and your book 28 years ago? I have been blessed to have worked in Mexico, Hollywood and around the world. I have won many awards for my acting and character portrayals over the years. But after reading your book, I have learned so much, especially about Back Story, character development and less is more. As you know, I have never studied acting, but this book will be my Bible from now on. You can only get so far with good looks. Ha-Ha.

I get numerous calls every week from people who are interested in getting into show business (you know how that is). From now on, anybody asking me about getting into show business, I will tell them that they have to read your book first.

Love you,
Your Hermano -Mike Moroff-Burciaga

Ken, **Mar. 4,**
2002

I do thank you for offering the workshop! It was an enlightening experience. It was also fun to meet new people and gain more insights from different perspectives. Please, do keep me in mind if you decide to offer other training.

I am really enjoying the book. I love the conversational style. And the content is so applicable to much of what I do and the manner and style in which I aspire to do it.

One of the assignments my class has to do for the end of the semester is to prepare an educational presentation about the ethnic/cultural group of their choice that would help others understand what it is like to be a member of that group. (It's a Multicultural Psych class). Following a very inspiring experience with Ken Farmer, I encouraged them not to prepare a series of "reports" on the group, but rather to create a character and tell that character's story, history, experiences, etc. (i.e., Back Story).

I think one key to truly respecting others whom we perceive as different, is connecting to the common, emotional-psychic human experiences. When we connect and identify with each other on an emotional level, we're able to respect the core person and are more motivated to use our "factual" knowledge to respond appropriately to any external factors.

Also, because students in the current era are raised expecting to be entertained, I think they learn (vs memorize) some material better if it is entertaining. Also, so many of our students at TAMU-CC work full time, have families...are very busy and don't have the proper leisure time to balance

their lives. Entertaining learning experiences are valuable on a variety of levels. I'm not saying every class period must be a dramatic performance; however, I do feel inspired to use a variety of creative tools that will facilitate true learning that the class participants will remember beyond the final exam.

I initially began to consider learning from experts in the acting field when I was talking to a young woman about a year ago who teaches children and adolescents singing. She said she helps them get over their performance jitters by teaching them acting first. That's something I've kept in the back of my mind. When called upon to teach, present, etc. I usually manage my jitters well enough to do the job required and receive positive feedback; however, I'm aware of potentially being able to do so much more if some of the energy I expend managing & masking anxiety were freed up to "just go with the flow and do it". At times, I've had those peak experiences where the presentation just flowed effortless and entertainingly from somewhere deep within (or without) me. And it was pretty awesome! That's when teaching/educating is really, really fun--like play...

Anyway, thanks again for offering to share your gifts and wisdom with others. I feel privileged to have been able to learn from you. The experience has, and continues to be, truly inspirational.
Best wishes and expectations,

Yolanda Harper-Ray

Ken,

I have always known that what you teach us in class is highly valuable. I guess I didn't realize how valuable until I started working on this student film. Putting everything you teach into practice for a project is great. I would not have known where to start when first handed the script if not for you.

At our first rehearsal I was the only one who had learned the script and no one could believe that I "knew all my lines" (and their's too). Doing a backstory has also helped me so much with acting. I realize that without the knowledge you have passed to us, I would be completely lost and clueless in this entire industry. Don't know where I'd be if I hadn't met ya. Just wanted to say thanks.

Love,
Kelly Carmichael - Actress, Los Angeles

Ken,

I learned more last night than in 6 months doing theater! I got home from class last night and my mind was racing. I couldn't get to sleep...So I finished the entire book...Still couldn't sleep. Did some of the exercises...Scanned through the emotions I wasn't familiar with. Still couldn't sleep...Then started to read the book again... Finally got to sleep some time around 4am. Just wanted to say thanks for taking me on. It's going to be a real privilege to be in your class. Not only will I learn from you, but also many of your students...Wow...What a talented group of people!

Shane Hamlin - Actor - Dallas

Ken,

I just wanted to tell ya I miss being in class and I am ready to be able to come more. And also I can't imagine what I would be doing now had I never met you. (Maybe medical school-ha ha) what I am trying to say is THANK YOU not only for being my friend but an amazing mentor and teacher. You are appreciated! And last I thank you for allowing me to feel the way I do on set, the way I feel my characters, the way the backstory takes over. Thank you for feeding my passion and making it something I can continue doing!

LOVE, ERYN BROOKE - Actress, Austin

Ken, I know I keep thanking you after everytime I take your class, but I just feel the need to do so! Thank you for last night's class!!! Even though I feel very green compared to others in the class, you have a way of making people feel comfortable for where they are, but push them to go further. Though acting for me (and probably everyone else, for that matter) can be frustrating, your approach is very motivating. I hope to be able to make you very proud some day!

Elizabeth de Moraes - Actress, Dallas

Hello Ken,

I received your book, "Acting is Storytelling", a while back now. I have read it a few times from beginning to end--so far! Your book has clarified a lot of things for me and confirmed some things I have done at times intuitively but then stopped doing (but now have gone back to doing). You have given me a lot of ideas. Thanks so much. I know you

live in TX, but do you ever do workshops here in LA? I sure would like to study with you if I ever got a chance.
A.J. - Los Angeles, Ca.

Hi Ken,

Happy New Year! Well I just wanted to share with you on what I experienced with your Line Learning Technique from your book, "Acting is Storytelling". Wow! amazing. I actually know the story and the dialogue. The test was when my scene partner and I got together to do a sit down line reading and I was amazed. There is still a lot for me to learn and it takes practice. I work on imagery daily and visualization. The play that I am working from is called Let Us Be Gay. My character is Kitty. It's an exercise and I am just having fun with it. I am so thankful for your book because I have a guideline to follow that WORKS. I did do a back story on my character which I have never done before in my life and that was really effective. That is something also that I have to practice to make a strong and effective back story. I refer to it as much as I can as well as your book. I am really blessed to have found you.

Thanks,
Kim Simon

Ken,

Well, hello, Ken, I just finished reading your book. Man, I gotta say, I've been an actor for over 40 years, and I still gained valuable insight, motivation and a deeper understanding of our craft from the reading.

Congratulations, ole son, and you keep on keeping on with your dedication and teaching. Anyone who studies with you is lucky to have you. A man who gives back to the acting community, who ask for little in return, but that does it with passion or not at all!

Cheers, Ron Becks - Executive Producer/Actor, Los Angeles, Ca.

COMMENTS FROM FIRST SCREENING OF "ROCKABILLY BABY" May 29, 2008

Written and Directed
By
Ken Farmer

(All the leads in "Rockabilly Baby" came from my PAG acting class.)

Leslie Jordan, Writer of the stage play, "Rockabilly Baby".

Ken... I cannot tell you how impressed I was. What I noticed that I had never noticed before was what an amazing "character study" the piece is. Those actors gave such fully realized performances that you saw the "wants and the dreams" of each actor in a very vivid, clear cut way. It really is a beautiful marriage of writing, directing and acting. Had any one of us not done our job to it's fullest (since there really is not a lot of action) the whole thing would have fallen on it's face. That is always the biggest concern, I think, when taking a theatre piece to film... the lack of action. The "rule," if there is such a rule, is that on stage you TELL the story but on film you must SHOW the story. Well, you did both and it worked. Most importantly, IT WORKED.

Thank you and thank your cast. I tell you what, those boys sure ain't hard on the eyes either. I am an aging homo who has been blessed with a deep appreciation for BEAUTY and watching that film was like going to a FINE ARTS MUSEUM!!! Love. Light.
LESLIE JORDAN -

Dear Ken,

As I sat there watching it unfold I felt privileged and grateful to be there. Most of the time on the edge of my seat.

What a splendid job by all concerned! I was riveted. And no car chases, extravagant scenery, nudity, blood and violence, just consummate, compelling performances by extraordinarily talented actors.

If you had the world to choose from you could not have come up with a better cast. Great job of casting and kudos to you for staying out of their way and letting them rock and roll. The best kind of directing. My hat is off to you and your "kids," Denton, Todd, Brandi, Kelly, Maeghan and all the rest. Denton, Todd and Brandi carried the piece like the giant stars they are bound to become. Didn't get to meet Todd but hope that I will sometime. Congratulations to Buck for having the good sense to support y'all. I was also impressed with the quality of the digital photography. Pretty neat.

God bless you and the best of "British Luck" to all of you. Thanks for a great experience. Sincerely,

ALEX CORD (www.alexcord.com)

Linda Dowell, SCREEN ACTOR'S GUILD
Hello, Ken & Buck.

I just wanted to extend a big JOB WELL DONE for the wonderful film you have created. I was very impressed with the performances and appreciate the opportunity to experience the sneak peek. You've made the stars of Dallas shine!

Linda Dowell / SCREEN ACTORS GUILD - Regional Branch Division Executive Director

From Linda McAlister, Linda McAlister Talent

Texas talent totally SHINED and glittered in this excellent character driven film: talent, director, crew, music, equipment, locations, wardrobe. A total top shelf production that truly makes us all very proud. AND with no nudity, no action, just crisp, sassy dialogue. Some clichés, yes, but it was the era that clichés were created. Fun times.

I do hope you can arrange a screening for the film critics. This is worth it! No major stars are in it. <u>They aren't needed</u> and I don't think anyone will care since all performers in this little gem of a movie are star quality.

This Texas is very proud of what our industry can do! With the right resources, it's magic. Truly.

Ken, you did an incredible job! Please do keep us posted for future screenings and developments.

Staying tuned!
Linda
Linda McAlister Talent

BLACK EAGLE FORCE - Eye of the Storm

Marine & Air Force Pilot create *BLACK EAGLE FORCE.*

High-Tech Special Ops Force Defends American Shores in New Military Action Thriller novel.

Black Eagle Force is a top-secret, Special Ops unit of ex-military men and women created for its ultra-rapid-deployment capabilities and intended to operate outside of governmental restrictions. In *Eye of the Storm*, a fast-paced new military thriller novel by Buck Stienke and Ken Farmer, a border skirmish on a Texas ranch catches the attention of the DoD, and within minutes, the BEF is scrambled in their high-tech VTOL aircraft to investigate and to protect the United States border. Joining forces with the former Marine family that owns the Texas ranch, their mission deepens to preventing **suitcase nuclear weapons** from being detonated by terrorists in the United States, while struggling to penetrate a criminal empire on a remote, heavily defended island in the Gulf of Mexico. They are tasked by President Annette Henry Thompson to **sanction with extreme prejudice** the mastermind behind the acquisition of the nuclear devices, also a trafficker in drugs and human lives, and in the quest to accomplish this before Hurricane Ellen hits the island fortress, BEF finds itself challenged to live up to its motto: ***Semper Paro Bellum***—"Always ready for war".

www.blackeagleforce.com - *Black Eagle Force* can be ordered from the website and anywhere on-line. FaceBook Fan Page: http://www.facebook.com/BLACKEAGLEFORCE

BLACK EAGLE FORCE ENDORSEMENTS

Black Eagle Force: Eye of the Storm. Buck Stienke and Ken Farmer take an intriguing premise and run hard with it in their new novel, Eye of the Storm. From the rattle of 50s to the smooth whine of the engines on their near-future aircraft, the book sings with authenticity and action. Readers will lose sleep with this one - I know I did.

- Jim DeFelice, best-selling author of the Dreamland series and *Omar Bradley: General at War*

****

+5 Star Review of *Black Eagle Force: Eye of the Storm*: This well written and exciting adventure story is reminiscent of the Tom Clancy novels at their best, but this book has more action. The authors describe the battles and other exploits of a unique battle force in fascinating detail that draw readers into the clashes. Readers will react as they read and as they finish this action-packed drama: "Wow! When will the next book come out?"
Dr. Israel Drazin at *www.booksnthoughts.com*

****

THE BOOKSHELF DETECTIVE
Book Review by JOSEPH PROVOST: **5 of 5 STAR RATING**
I was the lucky winner of an advanced reader copy of *BLACK EAGLE FORCE* by Buck Stienke and Ken Farmer. I found it beyond exciting. From the beginning of this military thriller to the end, the reader feels like they're on an adventure. Stienke and

Farmer start with Santa Anna's campaign in 1836 and take you through to present day in a way that makes you feel like you're reliving history.
Joseph Provost CWO 2 (retired)
Quartermaster Core

****

Finally there's an action adventure novel that actually walks its talk. In *BLACK EAGLE FORCE - Eye of the Storm* authors Buck Steinke and Ken Farmer have not only created a credible, highly kinetic page-turner, they have also set the stage for a classic series in the tradition of Tom Clancy, Ken Follett and Morris West. This book is an all out winner! I can't wait for the sequel.
Robert Joseph Ahola - Author, Playwright, Screenwriter
Malibu, California

****

If you're a fan of one-stop shopping, you'll love *Black Eagle Force: Eye of the Storm,* because this novel has it all: Nail-biting excitement, edge-of-your-seat action, fast-paced drama, and even laugh-out-loud humor. Believable characters, gritty, realistic dialog, and picturesque descriptions that provide a "you are there" sensation that will leave you wanting more. - Loree Lough, author of 80+ award-winning novels, including *From Ashes to Honor* [#1 in the First Responders series].

****

I just finished *Black Eagle Force*. I liked it very, very much, and I'm not an easy sell. I found it a quick, page-turning read. I recommend it to anyone who likes story, adventure, hard-hitting and constant action and many distinct, likable and appealing characters. Your devotion to detail, clarity and authenticity was admirable; as was the subject matter's relevance and topicality. It takes a point of view, and that is admirable in today's PC-culture. Agree with you or not, you attract us into your world--and make us see your perspective. That is the role of an artist. You and Buck deserve multiple pats on the back. Keep writing... and we'll all keep reading.

Kudos,

CLIFF OSMOND (actor/writer/director)

*Cliff wrote and directed the feature film, *The Penitent*, with Amand Assante and Raul Julia.

****

Black Eagle Force is a great read! I've read all of the current works by those who are in the best seller list repeatedly and *Black Eagle Force* smokes 'em all! The tale is dark, twisted and all too real in today's world. The best book I've read in decades.

This is a book everyone should read who wants to be informed and yet entertained at the same time. The pages could not be turned fast enough for me!

Doran Ingrham aka Plata (USMC Ret.)

****

I am John Eastman, author of Verdict! In Search of a Crime. I just finished reading Ken & Buck's *Black Eagle Force*. As far as my thoughts on BEF, I'll be simple; I'm impatiently waiting for the sequel.

John Eastman - (Major, USMC Ret.)

****

Growing up a military kid, I had people in mind to share BEF with before I even read it. I knew it would appeal to many of my friends, my father, and my stepfather, all of whom have been in the service, my father a career Navy pilot and weapons officer.

Several of my friends have Special Ops backgrounds and some are still active duty. I know they will love all the detailed descriptions of the advanced weaponry and aircraft operated by BEF as well as the adventure of their story. What I didn't know was how much I would enjoy the read myself. The Texas setting, the family values, and the action all had me turning the pages faster and faster to find out what would happen next and who would make it out alive.

Best wishes getting the book out, Ken! I know it will end up as a film in short order!
Stephanie Dunnam
Navy Junior and professional actor

****

I am very picky about the books I read but I have to say *Black Eagle Force* is one of my all time fovorites. I felt as though I was reading Michener, McMurtry, and Cussler all in one book and it kept me up way past my bedtime. There absolutely must be a sequel!!
Gary Hancock Pinkerton Special Agent (Retired)

****

Black Eagle Force is fast and action-packed, combined with a technical black ops style of butt-kicking storytelling. A+ from start to finish. Hard to put down. Bravo! Semper Fi!
Troy Phillips - Producer's Representative

****

I absolutely LOVED "Black Eagle Force." Honestly, I could not put it down! Great fast-paced read. Really like the beginning with its historical setting. This is not just a book for guys or military junkies. The ending was also a surprise. Can't wait for the sequel...and the MOVIE! Jocelyn K. White - "DESIGNING DFW" TV SHOW HOST.

****

Black Eagle Force: Eye of the Storm deals with a huge threat to this country of ours, addressing an issue I am all too familiar with in Arizona . Authors Ken Farmer and Buck Stienke have created an interesting ensemble – including a truly evil character who gave me chills, confronted by a hero and protagonist I would definitely respect. Climb aboard a Black Eagle for a thrill ride where the *Eye of the Storm* may be hitting dangerously close to your home.

Pierre O'Rourke
Author of *Free the Puddles* and *Driving Me Crazy*

****

The characters throughout were engaging, well-presented and memorable. I was also particularly pleased to have some "frailty" presented to some characters. The plot and setting were excellent and very timely. *Black Eagle Force* grabbed my attention quickly, involved me in the conflict and made me anxious and empathetic for the wonderful characters I came to know.
Joel Erik Thompson - JET, author of the *CAT* book series.

TIMBER CREEK PRESS

TIMBER CREEK PRESS

TABLE OF CONTENTS

Page

TIMBER CREEK PRESS

ACTING IS STORYTELLING©

BY

KEN FARMER

BASIC TENETS OF THIS SYSTEM

THE PAG SYSTEM©

STORYTELLING IS DONE THROUGH CHARACTERS

STORYTELLING IS THE OLDEST FORM OF COMMUNICATION KNOWN TO MAN

THE ACTOR'S FIRST RESPONSIBILITY IS TO

THE STORY

THE ACTOR'S SECOND RESPONSIBILITY IS TO *USE HIS IMAGINATION* TO CREATE HIS CHARACTER

THE ACTOR'S THIRD RESPONSIBILITY IS TO LEND THE CHARACTER HIS EQUIPMENT

<u>THEN GET OUT OF THE WAY AND LET THE CHARACTER TELL THE STORY</u>

THE ACTOR'S <u>ENERGY</u>, ITS USAGE, HIS ABILITY TO <u>VISUALIZE</u> WITH <u>POWER</u>, TO <u>LISTEN</u> AND HIS KNOWLEDGE OF <u>EMOTIONS</u> IN PLAYING THE MOMENT ARE HIS MOST IMPORTANT TOOLS IN TELLING THE <u>STORY</u>.

THE SINGLE MOST IMPORTANT INGREDIENT IN ACTING IS: <u>PASSION</u>!

PAG ACTING SYSTEM

Created and Developed By KEN FARMER

CHAPTER 1 - WHAT IS ACTING?

This is a question I ask each new acting student at the beginning of class. I get every type of answer one can imagine; from *"Being someone else", Playing a character," to "Being real".* So far no one yet has gotten it right. I ask them next: *"What is a novel?"* After a few hints they eventually say; *"A story?"* Then I ask; *"If a novel is a story, then what is a stage play?"* They hesitatingly answer; *"A story."*

WHAT IS A SCREEN PLAY?

They answer; *"A story."* And what is a commercial? They answer; *"A mini story." "If all these things are stories, then who is telling the story?" "The actor?" "Wrong." "The writer?" "Wrong." "The characters?" "Bingo".* The story is told by the characters and since we, as actors, are portraying (acting <u>*as*</u>, not like) the characters, could we not say that *acting is storytelling*? The look that comes over their faces when they figure out what acting really is, is classic, it should be photographed. (I'll do that one day)

ACTING <u>IS</u> STORYTELLING:

Is, always has been and always will be. That bears repeating: ACTING IS STORYTELLING; is, always has been and always will be.

NOTES

When actors realize what acting really is and what it's all about, I can see the light come on in their eyes at the *simplicity* of it. *Acting is Storytelling.* Storytelling is the oldest form of communication/education/healing in the history of mankind, dating back to the *"storyteller"* (the shaman) around the campfires of prehistoric or primitive villages. The stories painted or drawn on the walls of caves in petroglyphs, on animal skins and in the *oral tradition*, were man's first form of education, communication, entertainment and healing, far predating the written word.

The Twelve Tribes of Israel used the *"oral tradition"* for centuries in passing down the parables of the *Creation* and *Noah's Flood.* It was not until King Solomon decreed that these stories be written down, that we had any records from which much of the *"Old Testament"* was taken. We, as actors, have a responsibility to carry on this tradition, yes, in fact, mankind has a *"need"* for *"storytellers"* that is almost as great as his need for love.

HOW DO YOU TELL THE STORY?

The actor must first ***know the story***; in fact, under The PAG System©, knowing the story is the New Age Actor's *first responsibility.* Notice I did not say *"plot"*; there is a great difference between story and plot. He must know each event down to the tiniest detail in proper sequence *(all stories have a sequence of events; one thing happenend first, one thing happened second, etc.).* He then must ***create*** his character. Stories are told by and through the characters by *visualization and* by *coloring* the *events* with *emotions.*

NOTES

Acting, (Storytelling) as an art form, is evolving and freeing itself from the dogmas, rituals, routines and authorities of the past. Stanislaviski's Method, Meisner's Technique, Chekhov's Approach and the other psycho-intellectual forms of acting have become antiquated, limiting, cumbersome, ponderous, clumsy, stiff, *dangerous to the actor*, confusing, basically ineffectual and *stifling to creativity*. (Other than these problems, the old methods are probably all right.)

OLD METHODS:
In these old methods, (which were based on audience tastes and preferences *at the time*; theater has *always* been an extension of a culture's attempt at self analysis) things were done according to formula, the *"guideposts",* or *"gote sheet"* (gag... puke), even to the archaic *planning* of gestures or movements and the *choreographing* of emotions. Choreographing of actions, gestures and/or emotions, to me, is like painting a picture *"by the numbers",* it is not *"creating"* and playing the moment. I was originally trained in the "Method", in college, but soon abandoned it for Meisner and eventually trying or experimenting with most of the other so-called psyco-intellectual forms that evolved from the "Method" in my thirty-five year career (so far) as a professional actor; I like to say, *"been there, done that, got the 'T' shirt and now I wash my horse with it."*

"ACTING WITHOUT EMOTIONS IS LIKE AN EAGLE WITHOUT WINGS."

NOTES

PATTERNS of EXPRESSION:

Today, the actor or creative artist, must work out his own uninhibited patterns of expression, *get out of his head, create his character, play and stay in the moment.* He should never negate or resist an impulse of the *character*; *all* lines (or the emotional content thereof) of dialogue will cause the character to *(a) stand still; (b) move back; or (c) move toward.* The movements (toward or back) may be half an inch or half a mile; even if it is infinitesimal, especially on film, it is a byproduct of *listening* and responding to the other character's dialogue/action or your own character's. *"Listening is the single most important thing an actor can do during a performance."* [1]- (Meryl Streep) *"Don't listen to the words, listen to the person."* [2]- (Jack Lemmon)

Directors are learning (at least some are) that they get better performances *"when they set actors free, to give them openendedness (freedom to explore); create a space, or perimeter, where actors feel empowered and have room to let go and enjoy letting their creative juices flow." (James Cameron)* Every major actor I know or seen interviewed, has stated that they preferred a director who *understands the acting process* and allows them the freedom to create. A Director should tell the actor what he *wants from the character, supply the vision*, not how to do it. He is not there to give acting lessons; film making can cost twenty thousand dollars an hour and up (way up), he does not have the time.

---

[1] Inside the Actor's Studio - Interview with Meryl Streep - 2000

[2] Inside the Actor's Studio - Interview with Jack Lemmon - 2001

NOTES

"I don't look for a puppet or someone to recite the lines when I cast, I look for actors who can bring something special to the story, hopefully something no one has thought of yet. I look for creativity." [3]*(Ron Howard)* The professional actor *must* commit his creative responsibility to the *story* and to the *character*.

The actor, after learning and knowing the story, starts to *create* his character beginning with the given circumstances as supplied by the writer, inserting his own given circumstances, (visible physical characteristics he cannot change; height, weight, race, etc.; notice I did not say "gender", we have men playing women and women playing men, makeup does wonders) then creating a comprehensive *BACK STORY* of the character. Second only to *knowing* the story, the *BACK STORY* is the most important responsibility of the actor. Repeating: the BACK STORY is the second most important responsibility of the actor. With it, he creates a character that is *anyone but himself*, it is always a *fantasy character* from a creative imagination that is based on someone else. You can shape your character to *anything* your imagination can deliver. *"A man isn't an actor until he commands a technique which enables him to get an impression across into the heart of an audience without reference or relation to his own individuality. The better the actor, the more completely is he able to eliminate the personal equation." John Barrymore*[4] - On the flip side; the *poorer the actor*, the more he must rely on his own personality (personal equation) in his attempt to tell the story.

---

3 Inside the Actor's Studio - Interview with Ron Howard - 2000

4 Helen Ten Broeck: "From Comedy to Tragedy; an interview with John Barrymore." New York, *Theatre Magazine* July, 1916.

NOTES

PREPARATION:

The most important steps in acting lie in <u>*preparation.*</u> *IN PREPARATION.* It is the key to good acting; learning the story, researching and creating the character and lastly, learning the dialogue. All of these things *must* be done before you can even *approach* the stage or set. The actor cannot begin to "*eliminate the personal equation*" in the absence of preparation. There can be no *creation* in the absence of preparation. There can be no *true performance....* in the absence of preparation.

"Once the Casting is Done, the Art Belongs to the Actor." **-Robert Altman-**

NOTES

CHAPTER 2 - THE BACK STORY

With the old methods, styles, systems and approaches, far too much emphasis is placed upon intellectual analysis; the analysis or interpretation of the story and the analysis or interpretation of the character; what's the subtext, what did the writer mean, what are my character's obstacles, what does my character want, who's helping the character, what is the character's objective, etc, etc. *Every step the actor takes toward intellectualizing the story or the character, takes him one step away from the story or the character.* You don't think about acting, you feel it. If the heart is empty, then the head doesn't matter. *Most actors analyze too much and create too little.* *It is better to eat your soup than to speculate on it.*

RIGHT BRAIN, LEFT BRAIN:

It's generally understood today about the function of our brain; the left side is the analytical or logic (linear) side and the right side is the creative or abstract side. The left is usually jealously dominant and will suppress the right whenever possible. The moment the actor starts to *think* 'what's my objective', 'what's the objective of the scene', 'if', 'what's the subtext', 'what's my next line', etc., he automatically and axiomatically *smothers his creativity*. Most people's brains have a great difficulty in transferring information from one side to the other. The thinking side is always *ego* based and is the side used when we try to "interpret or analyze"; the actor must learn to ignore the *"ego"* and allow the creativity to rise to the surface. The left side is used in preparation—the right side is used in performing.

"It is only when we lose all awareness of the 'self', that the character becomes alive." -(James Caan)[5]

---

5 Inside the Actor's Studio - Interview with James Caan - 2001.

NOTES

DRAMATIC INTERPRETATION:

"Dramatic interpretation is a byproduct of knowing. For this reason, interpretation is a *result*, not a *cause*."[6] When the actor ***knows*** the story and has *created* his character, ***interpretation will always take care of itself.*** Again: interpretation is a byproduct of knowing. The actor must read and reread the script (preferably aloud), many times as an *observer,* ***an observer****, not as a participant*, paying *no more attention to one character than another*, to fully understand and know the story and its *sequence of events; all stories have a sequence of events with a beginning, middle and an end.* (Anthony Hopkins has stated that he reads a script up to 500 times *before* beginning to work on his character.) Once the story and the sequence of events is understood, *and only then,* can the actor begin the work on the character's BACK STORY.

OPPORTUNITIES FOR ACTORS:

As previously mentioned, the actor starts with the given circumstances as supplied by the author and himself for his foundation. Back in 1985, when I was shooting "Silverado", I was told by Mark Kasdan, co-writer of the screen play, that *"Writers create opportunities for actors, we supply the bones or frame of the character and it is up to the actor to create the flesh, blood, skin, hair, eyes and teeth and to breathe life into the character and make him unique.*

---

6 Charlotte Crocker, Victor Fields, Will Broomall -"Taking the Stage" Pitman Publishing , New York Copyright 1939

NOTES

Writers have neither the time, inclination nor the space to lay out a character for the actor. If we did, a normal movie script (120 to 140 pages) would be longer than "War and Peace". That's why we cast actors who can create their character based upon their understanding of the story." "Don't ask me what I meant to express with my stories, ask yourself what they mean to you." - Eugene O'Neill

THE CREATIVE PROCESS:

The BACK STORY initiates the *creative process* of the actor (all creativity starts with impulse. *"Imagination and creativity are guests that do not like to visit lazy people."* - Tchaikowski) The actor creates (in *writing*) a complete biography of the character from birth up to the time the story takes place as well as a psychological profile. It is not mandatory to apply terms as *sanguine*, *choleric*, *melancholy*, *phlegmatic*, *Type A* or *Type B,* etc., although it can be helpful; it may also be beneficial to look up the *astrological* profile and the tendencies from the birth date (which, of course the actor usually has to create). Primarily the actor should be interested in what the character is like or what *makes him tick*. What are his goals, what are his desires, wants and needs in *his* life. What are his mores, habits, manners, lifestyle and values. What interesting things have happened to him in his life that makes him *unique*? How does he respond and deal with conflict, crisis, fear and love and why. (Commonplace is not interesting) He must even *create* anticipation or dread of future events for the character; what is the character looking forward to (or dreading), what goals (specifically) has he set for himself in his life, what does he anticipate is going to happen to him. *"Always give the character a secret that only he knows."* - Katharine Hepburn. And I have added: Always give your character a secret he knows about the other character(s) that the other character(s) doesn't know he knows.

NOTES

FROM WITHIN TO WITHOUT:

Expression moves from within to without or to say it another way, as within, so without. To quote Dion Boucicault, "The Art of Acting", *"... the study of character should be from the inside; not from the outside! Great painters, I am told, used to draw a human figure in the nude form, and, when they were proposing to finish their pictures, to paint the costumes; then the costumes came right. That is exactly how an actor ought to study his art. He ought to paint his character in the nude form and put the costume on the last thing."* [7] You don't build a house from the outside, you must first design and construct the frame and the last thing you do is paint it. *"Always work from the inside out; if you work from the outside in, all you have is a dry husk."* - Meryl Streep[8]. A *character* is a blank canvas upon which the actor paints all of the emotions, details, fantasy memories and characteristics at his command. *The actor is the brush: emotions are the colors; the character is the canvas.*

NOBLE WILLINGHAM:

Recently I attended a function for Noble Willingham, who was running for a seat in the U. S. Congress. In visiting with Noble, I remarked how much I liked his performance as General Tayler in "GOOD MORNING, VIETNAM" and he commenced to tell the story of how he got the part. (Noble is a great storyteller). He was called in to read (along with every other actor his age in Hollywood) for the director, Barry Levinson, and after the usual small talk, Levinson asked if he was ready to read and Nobel said, *"No";* Levinson looked rather confused and Nobel continued, *"I'm not going to read, but I do want to tell you about this guy".*

---

7 Dion Boucicault - "The Art of Acting" Dramatic Museum of Columbia University, New York, 1926

8 Inside the Actor's Studio - Interview with Meryl Streep - 2000

NOTES

Noble began to tell the life story of the character, from birth to his current tour in Nam, *his entire life*, and when he finished, He asked Levinson, *"Now, do you still want me to read?"* Levinson replied, *"No,... I don't think that will be necessary"*. Fifteen minutes after Nobel left Levinson's office, his agent called and told him he was booked for the part. Nobel had done his research and created the entire Back Story before he went in and had such a clear visualization of the character that there was no need to read the dialogue. Ahh,.... the value of the Back Story.

Research is, sadly, one of the most neglected factors in creating a BACK STORY. Many student actors feel they can *"get by"* on charm or wit, grit and bull shit (*this is just pure laziness*). This attitude becomes habit and the easiest way to *change* a habit is *not* to inhibit or abandon it but to *replace* it. Changing a habit <u>*does not*</u> begin with a conscious choice to restrict your body from responding in its old natural way, but to seek out or design new habit patterns for your character and make a *conscious choice* to *replace* the old with the new. The old habits remain within your own personality and the new habits are ingrained in your character, but horrors of horrors, it does require some *effort and work*.

COMPLETE CHARACTERS:

In order to create a *complete* character, you <u>*must research*</u> and look for or create new habit patterns for the character; even if it is only seeking out and talking to the *type* of character you have to create. I was cast to play the part of an attorney in a "Dallas" episode back in the '80's and I went to an attorney friend of mine and asked him about being an attorney, from an attitude standpoint.

NOTES

He said, *"Just act like you know everything".* That simple piece of research formed the basis of my character's BACK STORY. It is not always that simple; what if you had to portray a blind person, a doctor, a paraplegic, a policeman; (I even attended a "Citizen's Police Academy", to learn procedures and terminology) you have to *earn* the right to play certain characters. Remember, we are not analytical artists, we are not interpretive artists, we are **creative artists**.

"We can shape clay into a pot, but it is the emptiness inside that holds whatever we want." - Lao Tzu -

NOTES

CHAPTER 3 - MEMORIES

A BACK STORY can easily (and should) exceed 50 pages because the actor must create, as part of and in addition to *Research*, memories; *Assumed Fantasy Memories* for the character that have nothing at all to do with his own memories except for some physical memories. Physical memories are things the character can, of course, do physically; roller skate, ride a horse, swim, play baseball, tennis, gymnastics, etc. The actor must remember that whatever *physical* capability he creates for the character, *he* must be able to perform. If he makes the character a champion swimmer and he (the actor) is afraid of the water; he has a problem. The actor should always be equal to or better than his character in physical capabilities; he can go downhill to the character, but the character can't go uphill to the actor (unless special effects are used).

PHYSICAL MEMORIES:

Physical memories can also include injuries to the character. (1) If the *actor's* "given circumstances" includes a physical impairment, (a bad knee, a missing finger, visible scar, etc.) he must create a "physical memory" for the *character* justifying the limp or the loss of the digit with the causal factor *different* from his own. (2) The actor can *create* other injury memories that are not necessarily physically visible; a broken arm from falling off his bicycle at the age of ten, for example. (3) The actor can create a physical infirmity like being crippled *if* it also creates an *internal* conflict (the best conflict of all) for the character. Billy Bob Thornton created such a situation in his BACK STORY for his character of Dan Truman (the Flight Director at NASA) in the film, “Armageddon”. He related the information in during a guest interview on "The Jay Leno Show", promoting_the release of the film.

NOTES

Billy Bob said he *"...created in his BACK STORY, a burning desire for the character, since childhood, to be an astronaut, but he also* <u>*created*</u> *his character a cripple from birth".* This set up a tremendous internal conflict within his character, making him original and very unique; *"I want to go into space, but I can never physically qualify, so I worked my way up to become Flight Director at NASA, to be as close to the space program as possible and vicariously live my dream."* [9] His performance stole the show, in my opinion.

KNOWLEDGE MEMORIES:

Knowledge memories are anything the *character* knows or has learned in his life and even what he wants to learn. What were/are his favorite subjects in school, what were his least favorites. What does (did) he like to study outside of school, like a hobby; baseball trivia, paleontology, rock collecting, the occult, painting, etc. Unlike some Physical memories, Knowledge memories should have nothing at all to do with the *actor's own* knowledge memories. He can make his character a Quantum Nuclear Physicist and the actor may not know his butt from a gin whistle about a "Quark" or a "Positronic Network", but he should *research* the basics of the profession.

---

[9] Interview with Billy Bob Thornton - "Jay Leno Show" NBC, 1999

NOTES

EMOTIONAL MEMORIES:

Emotional memories are absolutely vital to the character in the development of the BACK STORY. Weak or shallow emotional memories set the stage for the actor to *"break character"* and use his *own* memories. Emotional memories (causal stimuli), must be painstakingly created if the actor is to avoid *"breaking character".* The actor must realize that his character needs a balance of memories, using the *"Yin and Yang"* principle, creating good or happy memories as well as sad or traumatic memories for the character to utilize in playing each moment and it is the *strength* and *clarity* of the memories that *keeps* him in character and in the moment. Emotional memories create the basis of the character's personality; how he responds to crisis, to conflict, fear, to love and to what *automatic choice*s he will make when playing the moment (A character's choices will always naturally flow from the character traits you establish in his Back Story). Personality defining memories *usually* have occurred by the age of twelve. *"The response of the character to any given situation within the context of a scene comes from the preparation of the Back Story."* - Peter Brown

FUTURE EVENTS:

Anticipation or dread of *Future events* is the final section of "Memories". Every individual has thoughts that constantly occur to them daily; "I have an appointment at the dentist for a root canal tomorrow, I have to get my taxes done, tomorrow is payday, I need a raise, I have a date tomorrow night, my daughter has a recital, etc.". Your character is certainly no different, he not only has a life (the Back Story) that precedes the story, but also that life must and will continue *after* the story.

NOTES

TOO LITTLE:

Everything the *character* has done in his life or anticipates doing, the actor must know and therefore has to *create;* the actor must decide what skeletons the character has in his closet, what things the character is most proud/ashamed of, etc. Once adhering to the given circumstances, the actor can basically play God, he can create any memory or thought for the character he chooses, there is no right or wrong, ***(there is only too little)*** so long as he *begins* with the given circumstances supplied by the writer. In order to become and be the character, the actor must know everything about the character and the beauty is that the actor gets to *create* it. You must know the character better than you know yourself. It is a *wise* person who knows *others*, but it is an *enlightened* person who knows *himself.* Most people, when they look at *themselves*, don't or can't see themselves as they really are; too close to the forest to see the trees, we are too *subjective* and *protective* about *ourselves* (ego). However, in creating a character, the actor can be *completely objective* and create whatever his *imagination* can deliver; it's like decorating a home from scratch with deep pockets. In a recent convesation with an actor friend of mine, David Harrod, ("Thin Red Line") he told me that Nick Nolte reported to the set with over *two hundred pages* in his Back Story. David said, *"with my fifty pages, I knew right away that I was underprepared".* Again, there is only too little.

NOTES

OLIVIER & STEWART:

Sir Laurence Olivier said in "Great Acting", *"I usually collect a lot of details, a lot of characteristics, and find a creature [character] swimming about somewhere in the middle of them."* [10] It is the character's *lifestyle* that dictates what the character's personality is like and what choices he will make and this is where the character becomes *unique and original.* Patrick Stewart is quoted as saying, *"I am an actor dedicated to transforming myself and to creating original pieces of work..."* A word of caution here; don't create a unique or original character for its *own* sake, the character must fit and flow with the story and the other characters.

JOINT BACK STORIES:

The actors should make *joint* BACK STORIES for the length of time the characters have been together in the story; how they met, what their relationship is, *common memories*; Emotional, Physical, Knowledge and Anticipation's, etc. You can remember them as, "PEAK" memories. **P**hysical, **E**motional, **A**nticipation and **K**nowledge. JOINT BACK STORIES are absolutely vital to the emotional base between characters.

AUDIENCE APATHY:

The thing an actor should hate and fear most is *audience apathy.* When his audience doesn't care about his character; love your character, hate your character or at least find your character interesting, then the actor has *failed in his creation.* One of the most talented and committed students I have been blessed to coach, Britt McEachern, told me she uses the *Internet* to assist in the creation of her Back Stories.

---

[10] Laurence Olivier interview by Kenneth Tynan, in *Great Acting,* edited by Hal Burton, Hill & Wang, New York, 1967.

NOTES

Britt has found a *Keirsey Temperament and Character web site", (http://.www.keirsey.com)* where she first took the test as herself and then takes it as her character. This practice can be a wonderful adjunct to creating a *unique* and more complete BACK STORY for the New Age Actor and it will also tell you if you have, in fact, created a *character* or were just fooling yourself. Kudos to Britt.

THE ZODIAC:

Britt also gave me a book last Christmas that can be an enormous help in creating your character's traits. "THE LITTLE GIANT ENCYCLOPEDIA OF THE ZODIAC", The Diagram Group, Sterling Publishing Company, Inc. (ISBN 0-8069-9529-7), see page 8. When you create your character's birth date, you can turn to that sign in the book where it lists all the Positive Characteristics along with all of the Negative Characteristics. Take it with you to auditions when you have to create a really quick Back Story. It's handier than handles on a jug.

EMOTIONAL CHARACTERISTICS:

The below listed characteristics are the *"What"* about your character; you must also create the *"Why",* by using *fantasy emotional memories* in your Back Story. This list is an adjunct to your outline for your character.

- Strengths/Weaknesses
- Introvert or Extrovert (Personality category or type)
- How does the character deal with anger?
  - ✓ With sadness?
  - ✓ With conflict?
  - ✓ With change?
  - ✓ With loss?

NOTES

- ✓ With love?
- ✓ With fear?
- ✓ With confrontation?

- What does the character want out of life? (Goals)
- What would the character like to change about himself or in his life?
- What motivates this character?
- What frightens this character?
- What makes this character happy/sad?
- Is the character judgmental of others?
- Is the character generous or stingy?
- Is the character compassionate, cruel or indifferent?
- Is the character generally polite or rude?
- Is the character easy-going or irritable/grouchy.
- Is the character self-conscious?
- Is the character confident or insecure?

It is usually easier to decide *(if it is not already stated in the writer's given circumstances for the character)* what characteristics or personality traits you wish or see for the character, *then* create the memories, lifestyle and or environment that made him that way.

"Until the Actor loses all Awarness of the 'Self', the Character will Never come to Life."
- James Caan -

NOTES

CHAPTER 4 - TRAINING ASPECTS

ABSORPTION:

As part of being able to create an effective BACK STORY, there are four major aspects of the actor's training. (a) Absorbing experiences (b) Mental discipline (assimilation), (c) Developing techniques of expression and (d) Commitment. *Absorption* represents the *cause* or source of experience; origin, genesis, inspiration, idea, conception, etc.

MENTAL DISCIPLINE:

Mental discipline represents the *on deck* or staging area between the inflow and outflow of experiences. During this stage, ideas are channeled, nurtured, fertilized and allowed to grow freely and then directed along the proper channels of mental and specialized physical activity (muscle memory).

TECHNIQUE:

Technique is the effect and result of all expressional training and creativity. It represents the forms through which expression reveals itself and is as unique as each individual. It is reported that Sir Laurence Olivier was once asked if he didn't believe in technique and he replied, *"No, I don't believe in technique, I believe in <u>great</u> technique"*.

NOTES

COMMITMENT:

Commitment is the glue that binds it all together. Without _total and unconditional commitment_ to the character, the story *and* to the training that acting requires, the actor is, and will always remain an *amateur*.

STUDENT OF ORIGINALITY:

Absorption also involves intelligence and _empathy_. Through absorption, the actor acquires a knowledge and conception of a characterization that is used throughout the BACK STORY. The actor *is*, and must *practice* being, a student of originality. He should constantly be on the alert for novel or unique experiences and expressions; to capture and remember the elements in each circumstance that he comes in contact with that makes them unique and absorb them for use in his BACK STORIES. *"Actors are observers and collectors of nuances of speech, attitude, actions and trivia that we use in the creation of our characters"*. -Whoopi Goldberg.[11]

SKILLS:

The actor who has skills in creating, developing and *absorbing original* and *unique* characters, lives longest in the memories of the audience. We all tend to rapidly forget the average or commonplace when it is in *competition* with unique and sensational circumstances; so, unless you are *"eye candy"*, and face it, most of us aren't (at least for long), it is your *skills*, not your looks, that will never let you down.

---

[11] Academy Awards Ceremony - 2000.

NOTES

DIGESTION:

After information or experience is observed and captured or harvested, it is digested through the mental processes (mental discipline). Mental activity (imagination) and *visualization* are the forces that stimulate, feed and direct the outpicturing of that which has been absorbed. Visualization is a direct byproduct of imagination; without an active and *practiced* imagination, visualization is virtually nonexistent and therefore visualization with *power* is impossible.

AFFECTED MEMORY:

I congratulate Michael Chekhov's deviation from Stanislaviski's *"Affective Memory"* (I actually refer to it as "*Affected* Memory") to create his *"Faculty of Imagination"* which was to become the foundation to his acting approach. Some of Chekhov's other approaches I no longer agree with because of the changing audience preferences, but I heartily encourage all actors to learn his techniques of developing and exercising the *imagination.* Sanford Meisner also falls into this category of evolution from Stanislaviski; he recognized the overwhelming danger to the actor's own *psyche* and his *creativity* by using his *own* emotional memories and created a system that led actors away from that minefield and into their imagination to create *fantasy* emotional memories. The major problem with the Meisner technique is that it is very clumsy, involves entirely too much intellectualism or analysis, creates an inordinate level of stiffness, stifles creativity and leaves the actor no choice but to play in his *own head* rather than the character, creating the epitome of what I call, *fence post acting.* It tends to make the actor a *craftsman* rather than an *artisan.*

NOTES

ANALYZING CHARACTERS:

Analyzing a character, or a scene, is *like dissecting a frog... the frog always winds up dead*. The more effort you put into analyzing, the stiffer you become. The more you try to peek into the writer's mind, the more your own creativity is smothered. Gene Hackman told me on the set of *Uncommon Valor*, "Kenny, acting is not a murder trial, stop looking for a motive. Don't analyze it. Let's go do the scene and see what happens."

EVOLVEMENT:

Stanislaviski was an evolvement from Zola, with overtones of Freud (they were buddies). Miesner, Chekhov, Adler and the others evolved from Stanislaviski's Method and so now *today's* audience is demanding that evolution continue whether we, as actors, like it or not. Audiences have always dictated acting styles; without an audience, there would be no actors.

OUTPICTURING:

Technique is involved in expression itself; through it, the absorbed concepts, enriched by the imagination and coupled with *intense study and mastery of the emotions*, are revealed in appropriate outward form with *internalized energy*. ("From energy, you can *create anything*, but you can't *create* energy." - Neale Donald Walsch) The actor must *reject* any external expressions that are not the result of *outpicturing* because these expressions will be superficial (outside in) and his behavior will then be false and not the result of visualization of his *inflow*. He should trust the *instincts of his character*, by never negating an impulse of the character that is based on inflow. *"Never feel your body, make your body feel you." - Kevin Spacey* [12]

---

[12] Inside the Actor's Studio - Interview with Kevin Spacey - 2000.

NOTES

We have been conditioned to *hide*; in fact all of our lives, we have been told by our parents, teachers or coaches; "don't do that" or "don't say this", "never let them see you sweat", "don't show your feelings"; everyone talks about feelings, but we are taught not to show them. These are admonishments that the actor must reserve for himself, *not his character*.

NO CONSEQUENCES:

This is one of the great joys of acting; no matter how vile, evil or morally destitute the character the actor is called upon to create and play, there are *no consequences*, no one gets hurt. The character can be as "bad", "evil" or "mean" as the actor chooses to make him and the actor can still walk away leaving his *character on the set* when the Director says, "Cut", feeling good about *himself.* Acting is, after all, only *pretend.*

COMMITMENT:

Commitment, being the glue or catalyst, is the one characteristic any actor must possess to the nth degree if he is to be successful in this business. Tom Hanks said recently on the "Regis and Kathy Lee Show", that *"it didn't matter if you were a major super star or waiting on tables between acting jobs, you have to love (be committed to) this Business."* [13]

---

[13] *Regis and Cathy Lee Show* - NBC Interview with Tom Hanks, 2000.

NOTES

Commitment allows, precedes and carries outflow; it *forces* the actor to the next class, audition or role. It is the apex of *focus*. *Commitment* to the character and commitment to studying and training should be the bywords of all actors. Actors must ask themselves if they <u>*want*</u> or <u>*need*</u> to be an actor. If I had to choose between *commitment* and *talent* in an actor; I would take commitment every time.

FOUR ASPECTS:

These four major aspects of an actor's training encompass every phase of activity in the creation, mastery and presentation of a character. Remember them as Absorption, Assimilation (mental discipline), Expression (technique) and Commitment.

***"Method Acting, like Mediocrity,
sees only Itself".***

NOTES

CHAPTER 5 - POISE

The actor must also have *Poise* or develop it. The actor's poise (equipoise) is a *balance* between input and output, between impression and expression. To put it in the computer age; output always equals input or garbage in, garbage out. The manifestation of expression or outflow will be no better than the input (inflow) into the BACK STORY and when inflow is shallow and incomplete, the actor will *automatically* lose poise and compensate by substituting his own *personal* emotions or actions, which means the actor has *broken character* and is playing himself.

SHALLOW BACK STORY:

Shallow and incomplete information in the BACK STORY will *always* cause the actor's *focus to fail* and the actor will slide off the icy road to the character and into the ditch of his own personality. The actor must know that a rich *and full impression* is always the first prerequisite to *complete* and useable expression. The broader, deeper and *more detailed* a given concept in the BACK STORY becomes, the more self assurance (poise) and the higher the level of consistent energy and *creativity* the actor develops.

THE FOUNDATION:

The foundation of poise is always complete and detailed knowledge of the story and it's sequence of events. Poise also implies complete absorption and digestion. This means the actor can not permit himself any *predispositions, intolerance, propensities, bias,* or *prejudice* in the creation and portrayal of his character. The story, or rather the responsibility to the story,

NOTES

can never be absorbed, assimilated *or* outpictured properly if *preconceived* proclivities, concepts, opinions and judgments are allowed to interfere. In other words, *"you"* and all awareness of the *"self"* (ego) must get out of the way of the character and let *him* tell the story. Knowing the story without your personal interference *(objective observer)* creates balance (poise). We have all seen a ceiling fan with one heavy blade; it wobbles. The more *you* interfere, with your *own opinions*, the more the character wobbles and the more it wobbles, the less poise you have. Another outstanding student of mine, Denton Blane Everett, was recently cast to play the lead in a movie, *Happy Birthday*, directed by Yen Tan. Yen had called me complaining that he couldn't find an actor willing to play the lead because the character was a gay porn star. (Permitted Prejudice) I told him I had an outstanding student I was sure would do it. Now, Denton is as straight as a Laser beam, but as he told Yen, "Hell, I'm an actor, I don't care what the character is." *Happy Birthday* won 'Best Film' at the 2002 Philadelphia Film Festival and Denton got a super three paragraph review in the Philadelphia Weekly about his outstanding performance. I think it's safe to say that Denton kept all awareness of "Himself" out of the way...the "foundation of Poise".

FACTORS:

The factors which can inhibit proper assimilation include, among others: (a) a personal or innate dislike for a concept or idea in a script; (b) an aversion or distaste toward the *type of character* the actor is called upon to create; (c) when the performance environment seems inadequate or is unpleasant as when it may be, *in the actor's mind*, too hot, too cold, his dressing room is not to his self stylized expectations; (d) the role is not big enough [vanity; I won't use the old line about small roles and small actors].

NOTES

TRANSMUTATION:

The actor must allow himself to be transmuted into the character by freeing *all* inhibitions or reticence he may feel toward the concept; he must be a *creature of putty* ready to be formed or molded into the *character* through the freedom and creativity of his *own imagination*. We are *paid* to create a character and tell the story as written, not to promulgate our own opinions. The further from your own personality (ego) you can create your character; the more *free* the performance becomes. The more of ourselves we allow in the character; the more we will protect that character and restrict any risks the *character* should take. It is when there are no *personal* risks to the actor (ego) and his psyche, that the character takes on a life of it's own. It is the beauty of *"playlike"*.

**Good Acting is Never Observed;
it is Experienced. - KF -**

NOTES

CHAPTER 6 - THE FOUR DIMENSIONS OF ACTING

Acting has four dimensions. The actor's personal equipment is (a) the spoken word, (b) the physical action, (c) knowledge of the emotions (which is sadly, most often lacking) and (d) the mind action or reaction. The mind is always active; the actor's mind, during performance, must, therefore, always be *focused* on the story and upon some condition or aspect pertaining to his character and to the current situation (moment); after all he created the character's entire life and personality. If the actor has created, absorbed and assimilated his BACK STORY and is constantly thinking and *listening* as, that's *as,* (not like) his character, his actions will *automatically/axiomatically outpicture* his state of mind. It is the actor's responsibility to *lend* the character his *equipment (instrument)... and then get the hell out of the way and let the character tell the story.*

PARADOX:

It is a paradox of acting that an actor must *create* his character, *be* the creation and be an *observer* of that *creation* at the same time and this factor of *tri-separation* is probably the hardest part of *real* acting that an actor has to learn (I call it *"The Actor's Trinity").* It is like being objective and subjective at the same time and requires entering another zone of awareness. *Creating* a character, *being* the character and being an *observer* of the character simultaneously sometimes feels like a contradiction inside a paradox wrapped in an enigma. Actors who fail to make the *separation*, are just playing themselves and shows the actor has *poor* skills or that the actor is just plain too *lazy* (or egotistical) to do the work required to create his character; no one ever drowned in their own sweat. *"Try not. Do, or do not. There is no try."* - Master Yoda

NOTES

REAL:

Many actors feel that by using their own personality and characteristics, they are being *"real"* or *"natural"* when, in reality, they mistake ego or vanity for genius and just lack the skills to make their *character real.* In my opinion, actors who continually play themselves tend to be boring and commonplace which begets the most fatal flaw of all - to be *uninteresting.* Watching some actors flounder about playing themselves over and over using their own self induced delusion that they are *acting*, is like wiping your butt on a wagon wheel,... there just ain't no end to it and it doesn't get the job done.

BEN JOHNSON:

There are exceptions to every rule, however. I refer to my good friend, Ben Johnson, the wonderful cowboy actor who passed away in 1996. Ben won the Academy Award for Best Supporting Actor (also the British Academy Award, Golden Globe, Natl. Board of Review and New York Film Critics Circle Award) for his role of *"Sam the Lion"* in Bogdanovich's "The Last Picture Show". Ben performed in 79 movies in his career and once told me, *"Kenny, I ain't no actor, I just play Ben Johnson,... but I play him better than anyone else I know."* Ben's personality was so unique and interesting, that that's what the directors and producers wanted him to play. Ben would never curse and this was a source of disagreement between he and Bogdanovich. The script called for "Sam the Lion " to be a trash mouth. Ben refused,... Ben won. Most of his dialogue was his own. Ben was, in actuality, a lot better actor than he gave himself credit for because he was always totally *committed* to the part and played a wide range of characters. He used to tell me that he always knew *all* the dialogue before they ever commenced principle photography; which tells me he *knew the story.*

NOTES

CHOREOGRAPHING:

Never make the mistake of planning (choreographing) physical or emotional actions/choices *ahead of your BACK STORY and absorption*; in other words, deciding if the character will lead with his head or any other part of his body, walk with a limp or get angry or sad on a certain line, is like buying cattle before you have a pasture to run them on. If you plan or choreograph an emotion; grief, anger, levity or despondency, etc., based on a line in the script, you are locking yourself into a situation that may *not* exist *in the moment* and playing in your head rather than being the character; you will be encouraging and even forcing the character to *not listen* because you have already decided what the character is going to do and that, in and of itself, breaks the moment and the entire scene becomes sterile. ***Never write an emotion next to a line in a script***. *"The worse thing an actor can do is to determine the outcome of a scene before you do it". -Jessica Lange.*[14] *"Listening is being able to be changed by the other person." - Alan Alda*[15]

KNOWLEDGE OF EMOTIONS:

You must never allow the character to ever *"go"* for the emotion, but rather be *open* to the causal factor (the stimuli) from the BACK STORY, in playing the moment. He should not *"will"* emotions to be produced, emotions are produced of their own accord as a result of the stimuli. Emotions are *'energy in motion'*. Your *knowledge and mastery of the emotions* will enhance the character's sensitivity and empathy to stimuli and *allow* the character to make *choices* that are *relevant* to the moment *at* the moment it happens, *not before*.

---

14 *Inside the Actor's Studio* - Interview with Jessica Lange, 2000.

15 *Inside the Actor's Studio* - Interview with Alan Alda, 2000.

NOTES

WORKSHOP:

Recently, in a workshop, I had given one of my most promising students a highly emotional monologue that she performed wonderfully as her character. Another coach later instructed her to choreograph her emotions by writing them on her script at certain lines. (Relax on this line, show grief at this line, be introspective here, etc.) There were *fourteen* emotional directions written on her two page monologue and the next time she performed the scene in class, she was so into her head in trying to follow these preconceived and choreographed emotions that she was completely flat and stiff (fence post acting). I asked her why she couldn't get into her character, and she said she didn't know, so I asked to see her script and noticed all of the directions written on it. (nuff said)

VISUALIZE WITH POWER:

If you truly absorb, assimilate and ***Visualize with Power***, the character and memories you have *created* (inflow), play the moment (just *let* it happen) and keep *yourself* out of the way, the physical actions and the emotions will follow (outflow) and automatically outpicture. *Think the thought, see the pictures, say the words, play and stay in the moment.* One of my most outstanding students, Eryn Brooke, (she also will be a major star) was told recently by a Producer in L.A. that she was a *"core"* actress; meaning she was so solid and comfortable with herself and her training (her core), that she could create any character without interference from herself. She never allows her ego to get in the way and therefore her characters are always interesting and "alive". Eryn has "IT" and "watchability".

NOTES

INTERNALIZATION OF ENERGY:

True application of technique leaves no room for any activity that is not under the actor's complete control. No single moment on the stage or set can ever proceed without a purpose. Many stage actors put too much attention into being *active*, (waterbug syndrome) often creating *"excessive business"* that has nothing to do with the matters at hand (the moment). In order to make the transition from stage to film or video, the stage actor *must* master the principle of *INTERNALIZATION OF ENERGY. Energy* is not always manifested in physical action; a film scene may require high energy but the camera never leaves your face in an extreme close-up (ECU) and the character staying on his "mark" and within "frame" is critical. Remember, the camera always *"sees"* thought. I sometimes refer to it as *"having a tremendous undercurrent of activity."*

INTERESTING:

I did a play in Los Angeles in 1986, *The Night of January 16th* by Ayn Rand; Susanne Hopkins, of the Daily News, wrote this review: *"... Gale Trumbeaux, who also directed, is Karen Andre, the elegant defendant who finds that indeed, the best-laid plans often go awry. Trumbeaux has such presence on the stage that she manages to be <u>interesting, even when she's just sitting there</u>.*

Her portrayal hints at mystery and it's that tinge of intrigue that makes Karen Andre just what she needs to be; fascinating. Matching Trumbeaux is Ken Farmer as Larry Regan, a gangster caught up in Andre's intrigue. Farmer's Regan is smooth, with a voice that rings with authority and controlled tenseness. He's got a perfect don't-mess-with-me attitude that sets the tone of his scenes and helps carry the Action." [16]

---

[16] Susanne Hopkins, *Daily News,* Los Angeles, 1988.

NOTES

All good actors have something going on *inside*, they have a *secret* that did not come from the given circumstances, but was created by themselves that pertains to the character's back story, rather than just sitting there waiting to recite their lines. On stage, the audience usually watches the person talking; in film, *they watch the person who is listening.*

BE WHAT YOU THINK:

This is the forth dimension. To neglect this factor is to make expression shallow, superficial, false, and unconvincing, it is *"fence post acting"*. The actor must always relate the action to its underlying *thought* from his Assumed Fantasy Memories. ***DON'T THINK ABOUT WHAT YOU ARE, BUT BE WHAT YOU THINK.*** Remember that phrase: DON'T THINK ABOUT WHAT YOU ARE, BUT BE WHAT YOU THINK. Thought is pure energy. Thinking *about* what you are is being on the outside looking in while *being what you think* is inside looking out. If you *ever* ask yourself the questions; *"if", "what if", "how", "how would", "how does", "what is",* about your character, then you are dealing with an incomplete and shallow BACK STORY, are *not* in character and are on the outside looking in.

"THE MIND IS EVERYTHING; WHAT YOU THINK,
YOU BECOME". - Buddha

NOTES

CHAPTER 7 - NEW SENSES

The actor must develop new senses. (1) *THE MIGRATORY SENSE.*[17] The actor must be pliable enough mentally and emotionally to imagine and *visualize* himself anyone and/or everyone. Therefore, every situation, every person is of interest to the actor. It is necessary to develop insight (empathy) into the feelings, thoughts and emotions of other personalities. To completely capture and understand their sensations, emotions, experiences, reactions and expressions, attitudes and thought processes; the actor must constantly migrate out of himself, observing, harvesting and collecting the experiences of others to create fodder (material) for his BACK STORY. (Walk a mile in their shoes; boy, that's trite, but accurate for the actor)

POWERS OF OBSERVATION:

He must develop his *Powers of Observation* (PO) when he is around other people; at the mall, a party, church, school, restaurant, sporting event or anywhere people gather. (It is often better than going to the zoo.) He should take notes or possibly use a small recorder to help record his observations. With *long training and study*, he instinctively learns to project himself while observing other personalities; how they walk, talk, their attitude, body actions, gestures and expressions, whenever he observes or contacts an interesting type. In this way, he will develop his migratory faculties and abilities. Sometimes in class, I have the students imitate someone in class, including me. It is usually a riot, but it forces everyone to learn to observe, because they never know when I am going to pull this exercise or who I am going to ask them to imitate.

---

[17] Charlotte Crocker, Victor Fields, Will Broomall -*Taking the Stage* Pitman Publishing , New York Copyright 1939.

NOTES

INITIATORY SENSE:

(2) *THE INITIATORY SENSE.* The Initiatory sense is used for what William Gillette called *"Creating the illusion of the first time."* [18] The thirtieth performance, rehearsal or take must seem as fresh, new and spontaneous as the first. Concentration or *focus* is the primary method toward this sense. When the actor is able to direct his attention completely and is constantly *focused* upon the character, the *character's memories and* the moment (suspension of disbelief), it means he is absorbing a deep impression of him from his BACK STORY and therefore, he is ***Visualizing with Power*** (VP). Every detail about the character, his memories, his personal characteristics and his environment and lifestyle from the BACK STORY must be absorbed and etched in the actor's mind.

THE BUBBLE:

You have heard of creating "the fourth wall" in acting to separate you from the audience; I prefer to create "the Bubble". The actor must visualize a complete "Bubble", with *every detail*, including all four walls, floor, ceiling, temperature, light, smells, furniture, pictures, etc., of the environment surrounding the character (see, feel, taste, smell and hear); this is where development, control and use of the imagination come into play. It may be 95 degrees in actuality, but the scene calls for 30 degrees; the actor, through *power visualization*, can literally create "goose bumps" on the skin of the character and cause him to shiver and shake with cold (commitment to the moment). We have all seen the special effects movies, like "Jurassic Park", etc., where the actors are running for their lives from dinosaurs. When in actuality, there are no dinosaurs, of course, and the actors are in front of a "green screen" and the creatures have been inserted by computer graphics (CG) during post.

---

[18] *The Illusion of the First Time in Acting*" - Dramatic Museum of Columbia University, 1915).

NOTES

The actors had to use their *imaginations* and <u>*visualize with power*</u> the creatures and allow their visualizations to create the desired *emotional response* to the moment.

FANTASY ACTING:

It is the actor's job to *"sell"* this moment to the audience, just like it is the stunt man's job to *"sell"* the blow to his jaw from the hero by his reaction when he snaps his head back even though the hero's fist or foot missed him by over six inches. If you want to see real *"commitment to the moment",* rent "The Bridge On The River Kwai" (Best Picture - 1958), and take note of Alec Guinness (Best Actor - 1958), later to be Obi Wan Kanobi in "Star Wars", portraying "Colonel Nicholson" as he is released from 'the box' in a Japanese prisoner of war camp at the River Kwai. The moment is truly a classic example of visualizing with power. I won't say any more in case you haven't seen this remarkable film. (Seven Academy Awards in 1958)

ILLUSION:

To create with effectiveness, the right measure of inflow and outflow with <u>visualization</u> (VP) guarantees maintenance of the *illusion* that the charactor is initiating an idea, emotion, word, expression or action for the very first time. A pattern I recommend is to change a detail in your visualization (inflow) of the character's memories from the Back Story such as the color of a car the character once owned or the type of dog he had as a pet or even what clothes he wore yesterday. These changes, although minor, will assist in keeping repetitive takes or performances (outflow) fresh. This sense must be active and in gear continually during the rehearsal period as well as repetitive takes or performances.

NOTES

AVOIDING CHOREOGRAPHED CHOICES:

The actor should avoid *choreographed* choices, movements, gestures, emotions or expressions like avoiding kicking a fresh cow pie on a hot day. The *character's* success depends upon an instinctive newness in everything he says or does. Don't confuse "choreographing" with *duplicating.* Once you find out what works in rehearsals or in the first take, stick with it because the character must *"duplicate"* with exactness, in all subsequent takes, (two shots, over-the-shoulder, close-ups, etc.) all of his choices, expressions, actions and emotions from the master take, but these duplications must be based on the *causal factors*, not merely *repeated* from the previous take(s). I actually prefer to rehearse like a dummy scrimmage, (football) three-quarter speed, just for timing and blocking and then allow the emotions to be released and flow and let creativity take over when you do it *"for real"* for the camera. Film differs from stage in that, among other things, subsequent takes must be identical, while on stage, each performance can be and usually is different, to a greater or lesser degree, than the previous or the succeeding presentation.

REACTION SENSE:

The BACK STORY lays the foundation for the character. Everything the character does or says is the outgrowth of that which has *preceded* it. The character must be presented as a continuous life that has had a previous existence and which continues after the scene is completed. Every line that the character speaks or every action must sound or look as if it were provoked (causal factor), rather than invented, either by the character's thought or *reaction* or by some other character's thought/action or by a condition outside itself.

NOTES

This is one of the reasons the actor must allow the character to listen and react rather rather than waiting for his cue to give his line. *"Hurry up and say your line so I can say mine"* is the thought that runs through many actor's minds as they play out a scene. It is a direct result of not *knowing the story*, only knowing their own dialogue and therefore just reciting *(fence post acting).*

HIGHLIGHTING DIALOGUE:

I consider it a cardinal sin for actors to "highlight" or "underline" only their lines when learning them. This very act forces the focus on only one set of lines at the expense of the *story.* **The PAG System©** requires that the actor "highlight" or "underline" only the *"important"* words (the ideas/events) of ***all*** character's dialogue. This procedure ensures that the actor is learning the *sequence of events* of the story; the lines will take care of themselves if the character just *listens.*

THE ART OF ACTING:

The art of acting is the art of reacting. Portrayal of a character never proceeds accidentally or willy-nilly; there is always sound and relevant motivation. This means that the character is always reacting to motivation *(motive + action = motivation)* supplied either through story or other characters (playing the moment and feeding off of their plate) and his own Back Story. In every case, *speech, gestures, emotion, expression and movement* is the result of a ***cause***; it is the response to something that requires action, but it is *never* choreographed.

NOTES

OSMOND & HACKMAN:

My first real professional acting coach, Cliff Osmond, hammered at me constantly to just *"play the moment and stop thinking about it"*. The same thing was said to me by Gene Hackman on the set of *Uncommon Valor*, *"Kenny, just create your character, and quit trying to analyze what's going on. Just* ***create*** *your character and let's go do the scene and see what happens; don't think about it, just do it. This is not a murder trial, don't look for a motive."* I got a pretty good education in acting from college... It took me years to get over it.

ACTOR'S SHUFFLE:

Many neophyte or amateur actors somehow feel (or maybe it's just nerves), that they have to move *during a scene*, they dance around, move back and forth, even while doing their own lines. We call this the *"actor's shuffle"*. Pay attention to the *character's* impulses, *don't move unless there is a reason to move* and if it's nerves, it's because you don't *know the story*.

WRITING A BACK STORY:

One of the great advantages, and I believe a *necessity*, of *writing* a BACK STORY for film work is films are almost never shot in sequence. You may shoot the middle first, the ending second and the beginning last. This format is done for logistics, of course. There may be an elapse of *weeks* between your entering a door from outside until the actual continuing interior scene is shot. Hopefully, your character has changed or made some transitions from the beginning of the story to the end and it is imperative to know where the character is in his development at all times.

NOTES

PETER BROWN:

One of my best friends, Peter Brown, (Star of the *Lawman* and *Laredo* series, over three thousand episodes of soaps and a plethora of movies.) told me he writes his BACK STORY on the backside of the pages of his script so he can refer to it easily on set and know where his character is in what ever scene is scheduled or *covered* on any given day.

COVER SET:

Many times, the actor can prepare for the outdoor scene that is listed on his "Call Sheet", only to have to go to a "Cover Set" (interior) because of weather and there *can be* major differences in his character. The BACK STORY is the actor's *road map* to the character. This is why, in my opinion, film acting is more difficult than stage acting; in stage acting the character proceeds in his development in an orderly fashion, in sequence, as it were; while in film, the actor must be prepared to play his character in a non-sequential fashion, most of the time very haphazardly (Chinese fire drill). The character may have to do a scene that enacts witnessing the death of his child in the morning and in the afternoon be tucking the child into bed and reading him a story. In the absence of a highly detailed BACK STORY, the character can become very lost and *unconvincing.*

NOTES

MIMETIC SENSE:

Mimesis, (to imitate) according to Aristotle, is the outpicturing of a person's mental state. Every actor demonstrates, with his body (instrument), the results of what's going on in his mind; *for the body is an instrument of the mind, so let the mind control the body, not the body control the mind*. The body (this includes the face, of course) *expresses* the thoughts and emotions which take place within the mind. When the actor *is what he thinks* (from the BACK STORY), the body responds *mimetically* to that image of life that he is constantly ***visualizing*** (VP) from his creation. In acting, every thought, reaction, impulse, gesture and mood, no matter how brief, to have any *expression* value, must be mimetically represented, not just mechanically reproduced.

MOLDING YOUR SELF:

The actor molds himself with facility to the imitation of every character, he is transported out of *himself* to become what he *imagines (We are what we think.);* Chaplin was a master at this. A simple exercise the actor can do is; close your eyes and visualize biting into a really juicy lemon... All done? You will notice an instant tightening of the muscles at the back of the jaw, probably a squinting of the eyes, a pursing of the face and massive increase of saliva in your mouth as the *body* responds to the *expected* onslaught of the tart acid. All of these physical responses radiate from a simple picture in your mind. **Visualization** (VP) will always have a visible physiological appearance in the behavior of the character. You have lent your equipment to your character (mind, voice and body) and your voice and body will always outpicture what is in the mind*; "Your body doesn't know it's acting."* - Sigourney Weaver[19]

[19] *Inside the Actor's Studio* - Interview with Sigourney Weaver, Bravo Channel - 2001.

NOTES

EYES:

This "visible appearance" most *effectively* takes place in the "eyes". It has been said that, *"The eyes are the windows to the soul".* The actor must allow the audience or camera to *see the character think,* not just mechanically respond with some preconceived look, line, action or movement.

CONSEQUENCES:

The *failure* to realize the importance of the mimetic sense and a flexible, moldable, physical tool (the body) that mimetically expresses states of mind (VP) and character, (outpicturing) brings dire consequences. The result is a style of acting that colors every role *alike* and is commonly called "Method" or Ego acting, which means the actor is being himself and not the character. *"It is only when the actor loses all awarness of 'self' that the character comes to life."*- James Caan[20]

THE IMAGERY SENSE:

IMAGERY SENSE. Michael Chekhov referred to it as *"The Faculty of Imagination".* I just call it VP *(Visualizing with Power).* We are not analytical artists, we are not interpretive artists, we are creative artists... *CREATIVE ARTISTS.* Being an interpreter or analyzer instead of a *creator* makes the actor, at best, a craftsman, not an artist. The *creator* in the actor is far more important than the *craftsman* or the *artisan;* in the absence of the creator, these are <u>nothing</u> and it is the *imagination that reflects the creator.* The ability to VP is a talent that must be developed, just like a muscle that must be exercised; the *imagination* must be <u>*trained*</u> *and* <u>*used*</u> in order to function at *creative levels*.

---

[20] *Inside the Actor's Studio* - Interview with James Caan - Bravo Channel 2001.

NOTES

IMAGERY:

I believe that one of the reasons many younger actors (born after 1960) have difficulty in imagery, is they spent much of their formative years in front of a television. I read recently that brain activity while watching television was *less* than while asleep. I was born in 1941 and it was not until 1953 that we got a television. Until that time my brother and I were read stories ("Swiss Family Robinson", "Paul Bunyon", "Treasure Island", etc.) by our mother each night before bed time. We also listened to programs on the radio, such as *The Green Hornet*, *Fibber McGee and Molly*, *Lux Theater*, etc. We developed the power of visualization from these programs and stories. We could see in our mind's eye the stories unfold from the books Mother read and from the radio shows. I still like to listen to audio tapes of old radio shows and I believe that the primary reason I am a voracious reader today is because I was read to. I make a practice of reading from a novel or screen play at least an hour before sleep each night to practice my imagery skills and because I just plain enjoy it.

PRACTICE:

Actors *must* practice daily using the IMAGERY SENSE, like reading with *visualization*. People who exercise their muscles are "body building"; actors must exercise their imagination and visualization skills; this can be called *"talent building"*. Vincent Ryan Ruggierro in, "The Art of Thinking", says; *"Studies confirm that most people behave unimaginatively not because they lack imagination, but because they fear ideas that differ from the norm, ideas that raise eyebrows. They do themselves a great disservice because <u>creativity depends on Imagination</u>."* [21]

---

[21] Vincent Ryan Ruggierro *The Art of Thinking: A Guide to Critical and Creative Thought (2nd edition)*. Harper and Row, New York, 1988.

NOTES

EMOTIONOLOGY:

EMOTIONOLOGY SENSE. Actors must "major" in *Emotionology;* a complete study, knowledge and mastery of the emotions. There are only two real or *Prime* emotions; *Love* and *Fear*. Everything else falls somewhere between or under those two and the actor first establishes under which of these base (Prime) emotions the subsequent primary and secondary emotions lie. These are the nuances of feelings. The knowledge and use of emotions is paramount to the telling of a story. Emotions (feelings) are the colors with which actors tell their stories and are the cause, not the result of good acting. The basic principle of dramatic art is "Empathy", which comes from the Greek *"en",* meaning *"in"* and from *"pathos"* which means *"feeling";* literally translated, *"inner feelings"* or *"Emotions",* with which we bring the audience into the story. If we know and understand the story, the only way we can relate that understanding is through the appropriate knowledge and use of the emotions. The actor cannot call upon his historical knowledge or memories of his own emotions; what if he is called upon to play a character like a John Wayne Gacy, a convicted sociopathic murderer and mutilator of countless young boys or Susan Smith, who murdered her two children by drowning them.

IMAGINATION:

It is *impossible* for an actor to express what he is incapable of experiencing *except* through an *educated* and developed *imagination.* It is the imagination that leads the actor to portray feelings he himself, in many cases, probably will *never* experience.

NOTES

"An actor must feel in order to act; but in order to act he must not feel!... How, then, is the actor to traverse his dilemma if he must be capable of the most intense feeling, yet in acting must not feel at all? Why, by the medium of the imagination." (David Balasco)[22] The actor must *know* the emotions in order to use and understand them in his imagination. *"Acting without emotions is like an eagle without wings."*

DICTIONARY OF EMOTIONS:

Appendix "A" is a Dictionary of Emotions (over 900 emotions listed and defined) The actor must take each emotion, place it under it's Prime (Love or Fear) then take the primary and secondary emotions, place each in order of or degree of intensity and write out the definitions. The actor should set a goal of studying twenty (20) primary emotions weekly until finished.

"We never do anything well until we cease to think about the manner of doing it".
-William Hazlitt-

---

[22] David Belasco - *The Theatre Through Its Stage Door* Edited by Louis V. Defoe; Benjamin Bloom, New York, 1969.

NOTES

CHAPTER 8 - ACTING, AN INSIDE JOB

Acting is now, and always will be, an *inside* job. The actor's tools through which he expresses his art and creation are composed of the breathing apparatus, vocal and speech organs, certain muscles, ligaments and bones that support posture and movement, facial tensions and expressions, etc. This same equipment is also used to sustain the actor's own life processes. Therefore, in addition to using his body as an actor, he must also use his body to live.

VITAL FUNCTIONS:

This means that the requirements of the character *must never* involve the deeper, vital life functions of the actor's body or the actor's *own emotional memories* (Affective[d] Memory). [If the only source of emotional memories are our own personal past experiences, are we really acting,... or just playing ourselves.] An actor, in a fit of passion or rage as the character, *must* remain mentally cool, alert, well poised, and completely self controlled throughout his performance. His *own* emotional base must remain whole. The audience may cry, boo or be so tense that you couldn't drive a nail in their butts with a hammer, but the actor, *inwardly*, must be serene, calm, cool, collected and controlled; being the *"creator, the creation and an observer of that creation at the same time."*

CONTROL:

When I was playing football in college, my Father used to tell me, *"Son, if you want to beat the guy in front of you, first get him mad"*. It became obvious whether I was playing football or later acting, that I had far more control over my body and mind when I kept my own *personal* emotions in check.

NOTES

STANISLAVSKI:

Even Stanislavski said, *" It is a queer thing, but when you really feel your role, the impression you make on your audience is poorer; when you have yourself well in hand and do not give your part everything you have in you, it turns out much better."* [23] (Underplaying) Joseph Jefferson said, *"For myself, I know that I act best when the heart is warm and the head is cool."* [24]

FEELING THE EMOTION:

My Father died in my arms when I was 25; he had suffered a heart attack and I was giving him mouth-to-mouth resuscitation when he literally breathed his last breath into my mouth. I was very close to my Father and it took six months (I threw up every day for three weeks) and countless prescriptions of Valium and Phenobarbital before I was able to find a *protected corner* in my mind to place the memory of his death. It was over 42 years ago and I am still affected by it. If I had to recall that memory every time I needed to express that level of emotional agony; they would have to find a padded room for me.

PERSONAL MEMORIES:

The actor who portrays his *own tiny experiential resources of emotion* from a personal memory (affected memory), rather than a *created fantasy memory* of the character; by allowing himself to *feel* and re-experience that emotion while he is expressing it, also allows his body and mind to be affected by the strain of that emotion and will find that he is *unable to walk away from it*.

---

[23] Konstantin s. Stanislavsky; *Art Notes*, 1877-1892. Moscow; International Literature.

[24] Joseph Jefferson, *The Autobiography of Joseph Jefferson,* edited by Alan S Downer. Cambridge, Mass.: Belknap Press, 1964.

NOTES

FANTASY:

I have a scene, that was given to me by my mentor, Cliff Osmond, I demonstrate in class occasionally in which I play a blue-collar father who comes home from work one day to find his wife in bed with their baby son. She had been nursing him, fell asleep and rolled over on him suffocating him to death with her breast. *"I reached out to touch my little Louie. (beat) He was so cold... I could feel... the blue through my fingers."* I have done that scene over 500 times and my character's visualization is so clear, that his voice breaks and tears roll unabashed down his cheeks each and every time he tells the story. Someone in class always asks after the scene when I "cut" and smile, wipe away the tears and point out the imagery I used, *"How do you do that,... just stop and carry on with class. That is the most emotional scene I have ever seen."* I just reply, *"Because it wasn't me and it wasn't real,... it was a fantasy. So it's easy to walk away from it.... and what if I had to do four or five or more takes from the top?"*

EMOTIONAL REALISM:

If it was my *own* memory, such expression of emotional realism would leave me drained, breathless, spent, and useless for the next sequence, retake or scene, not to take into account the *progressive damage* to my own psyche. The actor may greatly affect *himself* but not affect his audience at all; *"...he will inevitably derange his artistic mechanism and, rendering himself incapable of expressing anything, defeat his purpose."* (David Belasco)[25] The great stage actor of the late 1800's, Henry Irving, once declared, *"I never saw an actor lose himself, who did not instantly lose his audience..."* [26]

---

[25] David Belasco - *The Theatre Through Its Stage Door* Edited by Louis V. Defoe; Benjamin Bloom, New York, 1969.

[26] Henry Irving, Constant Coquelin and Dion Boucicault - *The Art of Acting* , 1926.

NOTES

THE METHOD:

Many actors who have practiced the "Method" wind up alcoholics, drug addicts, act like their bread's not quite done or spend half their life on some psychiatrist's couch. We have only to recall the well known story of Sir Laurence Olivier and Dustin Hoffman during the filming of "Marathon Man". In preparing for an interrogation/torture scene, Hoffman stayed up all night, didn't eat, shave or shower; upon arrival on set, ragged, odoriferous, unshaven and baggy-eyed. A well rested but confused Olivier remarked *"My dear boy, why don't you simply try acting?"* [27] The "Method" is far too dangerous to the actor and should be abandoned or replaced; it relies almost entirely on the *"personal equation"* and is a *poor way* to tell the story and in reality should be called *"Ego Acting". "At the feast of Ego, everyone leaves hungry."*. Method acting, like mediocrity, sees only itself.

REAL ACTING:

What a *real actor* should do is to portray to the audience's mind and sensibilities, the inner workings and experiences of an *Assumed Fantasy Personality (AFP)* with it's <u>own</u> emotions and memories. He shows the audience not only the *result*, but the thought process that *created* the result. <u>*Remember, the camera will always see thought.*</u>

---

[27] Laurence Olivier, *On Acting*, Simon and Schuster, New York 1986.

NOTES

ASSUMED FANTASY PERSONALITY:

We can draw a parallel between creating an Assumed Fantasy Personality and Multiple Personality Disorder (MPD) but without the *disorder*. MPD is a completely unconscious, uncontrollable disorder, even to the point of one personality literally having diabetes or blue eyes or other physiological characteristics while the base personality has brown eyes and no evidence of the disease or visa versa. (Showing the awesome power of the mind if we can ever learn to use it) Creating an Assumed Fantasy Personality is always *conscious* and under *complete control* and direction of the actor.

PSYCHOLOGISTS:

According to psychologists, human consciousness may exist separately from the brain itself; different personalities activate different regions of the brain, ergo, allowing them to form *separate* memory banks and actually create *new* neuro-synaptic pathways for the AFP. The complete control of creating an AFP lies in the BACK STORY, where we create *separate* memories and emotions from the fruits of our imagination; it is our road map or blueprint for the character. It ain't easy because it does require a great deal of *effort* and *practice*. You don't build a house without plans.

SACRED COW:

Stanislaviski died seventy years ago, it is time to honor his memory as sweet history, but also time to *bury him*. Stanislaviski himself said that his "Method" would evolve, as it did during his own lifetime, but there are those actors and teachers who still seek to cling to the *"old"* like a security blanket, rather than explore the new. Maybe it's time to jack the Method up and drive something else under it.

NOTES

Many of his disciples use whatever stage Stanislaviski was in at the time they were studying with him and this became their own approach that they and *their* disciples, for the most part, are *still using*. The "Method" is a *"sacred cow"* (Authority) to many actors; sacred cows... usually cause the most trouble... but make the best steaks. *"Every great advance in natural knowledge has involved the absolute rejection of Authority."* - Thomas Huxley. It seems to be an axiom that the less talented the artist, the sooner he forms his convictions and beliefs and the longer he blindly and stubbornly holds on to them. *"All empty souls tend to extreme opinion."* - William Butler Yeats

CHANGE:

Most people are dragged kicking and screaming into the future facing *backwards*, their eyes always on the *past, fearing the future*. If we are to grow, we must turn around. *"Fear always springs from ignorance"* - Emerson. Fear of change does strange things to us; it blinds us to logic and keeps us wrapped in the swaddling clothes of safe and accepted values. *It keeps us from exploring, learning and expanding. Fear of change is, in reality, fear of growth*. Growth always involves change. Learning always involves change and change always involves learning. *"It is what we think we know already that often prevents us from learning."* - Claude Bernard. You can't steal second with your foot on first. The only constant in the Universe is change itself.

"NEVER LET YOURSELF GET BETWEEN YOU AND YOUR CHARACTER."
-MICHAEL CAINE- [28]

---

[28] *Inside the Actor's Studio* - Interview with Michael Caine, 2000.

NOTES

CHAPTER 9 - CREATING AN ILLUSION

In creating the BACK STORY, the actor is creating a world of *illusion* and of *representation*. The actor deals with creating the character in terms of what it *seems, rather than in terms of what it is.* The magic that is true acting doesn't come from being *"real"*, but from the <u>appearance</u> that it's real. Actors don't portray life, they impersonate it. Thespis, (560 BC, from which our name, "Thespians" is derived) classified actors as *"impersonators"*.

THEATRIC ART:

The poet Goethe once remarked that *"Art is art precisely because it is not Nature."* The medium of theatric art is one of *pure illusion*; it is artificial and it is artificiality that we work with to create the *effects* of reality; it is a synthesis *creatively* presented in a structure designed to produce the desired *impression* on the audience to bring them into the story. It is when the actor lacks art to conceal art that the audience sees him to be artificial. <u>Theatric art is never realistic; it is always impressionistic</u>.

PARADOX OF ACTING:

A paradox of acting is that its most important element is not what is said or done, but the *implications* of what was uttered or performed. Every word or action contains an *explicit* or literal meaning,... and an *implicit* meaning; and the latter is always more important. Explicit statements present the "letter of the law", whereas implicit speaks of the "spirit of the law". In acting: "The letter killeth, but the spirit givith life." It is not *what* you say but *how* you say it. *"Words are the least reliable purveyor of Truth". -Walsch* [29]

---

[29] Neale Donald Walsch - *Conversations with God,* G. P. Putnam's Sons, New York, 1996.

NOTES

LIVING THE PART:

The actor must never *live* his part, since he must reserve his vital functions for the more important processes of controlling his techniques of expression. His body and mind are vehicles of artistic expression, but such vehicles must be maintained with equipoise and self control, with flexibility and *freedom to let the creative juices flow*. When the actor *lives* the part, he is being himself and has not created and absorbed the *character*. The actor must return to a capability we all had as children in our games, it was called *"playlike"*. Olivier said, *"The child finds it easy"*. He must remain upon a mental level that blends the three systems of communication - *thought, emotion, expression* - into mind action, which is always in supreme control of the characterization. Therefore, the actor does not reveal his *own* true nature, but that of the *Assumed Fantasy Personality* he has created and is portraying. The only limit is the actor's ability to *imagine, create* and *focus* and there *is no limit* to the extent to which these abilities can be *developed*. In reality, *we are our own limiting factor*.

LIMITING FACTOR:

Our primary limiting factor is our own ego. (The English word "Satan" is derived from the Aramaic word, "Satah"... which means "Ego".) *The further from your ego you can move, the greater the creative state.* Whenever you focus on yourself, you are axiomatically retarding your creative potential. *"Never let yourself get between you and your character."* (Michael Caine)[30] Our ego, our personal judgments, opinions and personal memories interfere with the creative outpicturing and any *consistent* openendedness. It is when we start to *"think"*, analyze or intellectualize, that we get into trouble, thinking is different than feeling *(feelings are the language of the soul)*.

---

[30] Ibid.

NOTES

Acting, as an art, is *felt*, deep in your gut, with everything you've got, you can't run it through a computer or analyze it with your mind. When we think (analyze), we shut down all creative expression. If you make a preconceived mental *choice*, then you are limiting your character to that and only that. Ego is linear in nature; when we create, we must be in the abstract mode. Linear thinking is our protection, but in acting, we need no protection. *"It's all about taking risks, revealing and exposing the character; but there are no real risks because there are never any consequences, it's a fantasy, so let go."* - Meryl Streep[31]

FUNCTIONAL CREATING:

Creating a character is, in a sense, like creating a fine painting in which each line, however delicate or broad, and each color, no matter the shade or value, serves a useful purpose in conveying the image, and no line or shading of color is without *function* in the final presentation of the image from the mind of the artist. The actor must utilize essential *details* of his character that serve specific purposes of characterization and emotions that are presented in nuances of color rather than in the primaries.

Each actor is unique; we can compare actors with painters for example. If you took ten artists out to a scenic woodland and asked each to paint what they saw; you would see ten completely different styles and interpretations of the setting. Actors are the same, we create characters based upon our own *personal creative* view and visualization of the character from *our* knowledge and understanding of the *story*. Ten actors creating the same character will come up with ten different BACK STORIES and yet they all started with the same *story* and given circumstances (setting).

---

[31] *Inside the Actor's Studio* - Interview with Meryl Streep, 2000.

NOTES

There is no right or wrong as long as each actor *starts* with the given circumstances supplied by the writer; there is only too little. One has only to rent the videos of Olivier's *Hamlet*, Branagh's *Hamlet* and Mel Gibson's *Hamlet*, to see the different personalities each had based on identical stories, identical given circumstances and identical dialogue.

OTHER ARTISTS:

The dissimilarity with the other artists; writers, painters, composers, etc., is *they* can erase or discard, but the actor is trapped or imprisoned. He will live or die with his creation and that is why there is no room for a careless, slackard, shallow and incomplete BACK STORY. The similarity should come in simplicity of expression; in the nuances used to color the character's personality. Compare economy of expression in acting with any of the other arts. True *economy in expression* and *simplicity* (underplaying or minimalism) are perhaps the key notes of great performances. As in all arts; simplicity *is* economy, but it is not meagerness. It's the little things that count. *"Entia non sunt multiplicanda praeter necessitatem."* - William of Occam (1287-1349) "OCCAM'S RAZOR" - Translated freely: *"One should not increase, beyond what is necessary, the number of entities required to explain anything."* The razor was intended to cut away muddles and confusions with little or no value. Knowledge is based on experience and self-evident truths.

"The Less Effort, the Faster and more Powerful you will be."
BRUCE LEE

NOTES

CHAPTER 10 - TECHNIQUES OF ACTING

IN MASTERING THE TECHNIQUES OF ACTING:

(1) The actor must learn that the single most important ingredient in acting is *PASSION!*

(2) He must always focus on the STORY and never the dialogue.

(3) He must be trained in habitualizing responses of his character so that they become automatic and instinctive reaction patterns; called *"grooving the channels of the mind"* or learning to direct each thought into its proper expressional activity for purposes of outpicturing.

(4) The actor must train his memory to absorb observed experience, record it in his BACK STORY and recall it when needed for a character,

(5) He must constantly practice and develop his powers of *Imagination*, *Creativity* and *Concentration* (Focus),

(6) He needs the ability to *Visualize with Power* (VP) the character he creates; he must *see* the character before he can *be* the character,

(7) He must practice daily, reading with *imagery*. (Seeing what he says.)

(8) He must learn how to create an *original* and unique character in his BACK STORY out of all the factors of his experience in observing character types and sometimes creating characters out of "whole cloth",

(9) He must acquire, through practice, the ability to *Create*, be the *Creation* and *Observe* his creation at the same time,

(10) He must learn how to *absorb* the character he has created and inject it smoothly into his understanding of the STORY,

(11) He must study, with a vengeance, the *Emotions*, for they are the very colors he must use to *"paint"* (tell) his story,

NOTES

(12) He must <u>*never*</u> <u>*memorize*</u> his dialogue, but rather *learn it* as he learns the story.
(13) He must *see* what he *says* in telling the story.
(14) He must perfect the art of *Listening and to allow his character to be changed by the other characters.*
(15) He must never listen to the *words*, but listen to the *person.*
(16) He must realize that the more he learns the more he needs to learn.
(17) He must be completely self disciplined/controlled at all times.
(18) He must never allow his own personality or personal memories to get between himself and his character.

MEMORIZATION:

When I was in High School, during the late '50's, My Senior English Lit teacher, Roberta Floyd, required that we all *memorize* the *"Prologue to the Canterbury Tales"* by Geoffrey Chaucer, *in* "Old English". I can recite it to this day and I memorized it over 40 years ago. She taught me a great deal about appreciating a good story. She wanted to be sure we got all the words right in telling a *classic* story. However, for actors, *Memorization* (I call it the "M" word; the most offensive word in the actor's vocabulary and is the kiss of death) involves the act of just <u>reciting</u> the words (fence post acting), which *does not* require an understanding or even *knowledge* of the *story,* whereas *learning* the dialogue does require an in-depth knowledge and understanding of the story <u>as</u> the character because the *character was there*.

NOTES

THE STORY IS THE KEY:

I was doing an ADR (Additional Dialogue Recording) session in Los Angeles (it is also known as 'looping') for "Uncommon Valor" and the director, Ted Kotcheff, asked me if I could do any other voices. Of course, I said yes. He asked if I would dub another character who was speaking Thai, now, since I don't know a word of Thai, he called in a young Thai lady to help me with the dialogue. She would say a phrase and I would repeat it (parrot) until I got it right then we would "loop it". I was extremely uncomfortable with the whole procedure until I asked her to completely translate the dialogue into a story; once I knew the *story*, it all begin to flow together. The *story* is always the key, no matter what language it is in.

FREE ACTING:

The actor must remember that *he* knows all the lines for all the characters from the script (or is supposed to) but his <u>*character does not nor does his character know what the other characters are going to say*</u>. He must allow the character the opportunity to *create* the words as he *listens to the other character(s)*, in playing and staying in the moment, with all the *emotions* and *visualizations* that a true knowledge of the story brings. The actor must recall, he is *lending* the character his equipment and now must get out of the way and allow the character to have his freedom.

FOCUS ON THE STORY:

When the actor performs <u>*as*</u> the character, he should focus on the <u>*story*</u> and <u>*never the words.*</u> If he is performing <u>*like*</u> the character, then, by its very nature, he will focus on the words and in so doing, will automatically lose focus on the story and will only be reciting (find me a fence post).

NOTES

With true knowledge and understanding of the story and a carefully created Back Story, *the words will always be there*; it is Free Acting. *"If you're practiced, rehearsed and thoroughly versed (know the story), you have something to offer. You know what the lines are about, but you haven't waited for the final, ultimate way of saying them or handling a single moment... take care of the play (story) and let genius take care of itself"*. - Sir Laurence Olivier[32]

"Shake the Dialogue 'till all the Words fall away; what is left is True Acting."
-KF-

[32] Laurence Olivier, *On Acting*, Simon and Schuster, New York 1986.

NOTES

CHAPTER 11 - STORYTELLING

MACDARA:

I recently was invited by one of my students, Bonnie Cochrane, to attend two one act Irish plays (the first of which she was in ["Shadow of the Glen", by J. M. Synge] and she turned in a very nice performance). The second was written and performed by the noted and award winning Irish actor, Macdara Mac Uibh Aille, entitled "The Voice of the Sea - *An t-Oilean a Bhi*". It was the most mesmerizing performance I have ever seen. Macdara played all the characters, using only one mask and voice and body changes, never moving out of a three foot circle and told his story with such *emotion* and clear *visualizations* that the entire audience was totally captivated for over an hour. I had the opportunity to meet him after the performance and was shocked to find he was only twenty-seven years old. I told him how wonderful his performance was, (a phrase I rarely use) that it was true *storytelling* and I was humbled in his presence. He was very modest in his thanks and replied; *"That's what acting is - Storytelling."* Well, kiss a fat baby, if that doesn't kill the corn ankle high, I can't tell you how blown away I was to discover that our philosophies on acting were virtually identical; *Acting is Storytelling*. He said; *"I wish that they had taught that philosophy when I was getting my degree in theater;... I had to learn it as a performer"*. An actor friend of mine, Vikas Adam, asked him if he had a script to the play, to which he replied, *"No, I just know and visualize the story and the words come out virtually the same each time I perform"*. An actor's focus should always be on the story (the Goal) and never on the task (how to get there). Storytelling is saying what we see.

NOTES

KNOW THE STORY:

Macdara also directed the first play, that Bonnie was in; the actors only had three weeks to learn the play and that included learning the Irish dialect of the turn of the century. Bonnie was having a confidence problem with the words and Macdara told her; *"Don't worry about the words, you know the story, just tell it".* *"Words are the least reliable purveyor of Truth".* - Neale Donald Walsch [33]

THE ART OF STORYTELLING:

Sometimes the actor must rise to the level of the words and sometime he must rise *above* the *words* in telling the story. *"In acting, dialogue or words are like a clay pot, it's what's inside that's important."* This is the art of communication, of persuasion, or to put it another way, acting is the *art* of *STORYTELLING.* (We think in metaphors, but communicate with stories.) Don't *think* about it, just do it! Storytelling is seeing what you say and of making sure your *eyes and mouth match. Good storytelling (acting) comes from the heart, not the head. Talent* is the ability to perform a task *without* thinking about it.

THE PAG SYSTEM:

The PAG System© is the *"how to"* of *STORYTELLING*; it is definitive acting; based on thirty-eight years of *actual practice* on set or stage, as a working actor, not some class room theory devised. The "System" is extremely simple in concept (Occam's Razor); there is only one drawback (for some people), the actor has to work his butt off to *learn* and *practice* his skills.

---

[33] Ibid

NOTES

WORK ETHIC:

The hallmark of a true actor *is* his *work ethic* (commitment) and a never ending desire and recognized *need* to learn. You will never *master* the art and craft of acting, no one ever has or ever will. *"Wisdom grows in direct ratio to one's awareness of his own ignorance."* The actor should try to learn something every day about the craft and art of acting (STORYTELLING), and the more he learns, the more he will find out he needs to learn. If he is ill, he sees a doctor, if his computer crashes, he finds a technician; so it is with acting. When learning the craft of acting, the actor should seek the council of a veteran teacher who, if preferences are to be had, is also an *experienced working actor.* Would you want to learn to fly an aircraft from someone who had never flown? And don't give me this crap about flying an airplane is taking your life in your hands; *acting is your life,* or should be, if you're in this business. Treat it as such.

SCIENCE AND ART:

A novice cannot begin to master the techniques of good acting with a few lessons or much less by reading a few books or essays on the subject, acting is like playing music or painting a picture, it is immediately a science *and* an art. It is a science in its learning and an art in its practice and practiced according to the rules of discovery and *experience*, not theory devised. The word "science" from Latin, *scientea - "methodological activity, discipline, or study. An activity regarded as requiring study and method; knowledge gained through experience."*

NOTES

TALENT:

The one thing that cannot be given or taught by *any* teacher, is the *talent to act*; one either has it or doesn't (in varying degrees). It's the same with the ability to sing, paint or write; these arts are all taught to those who have a God given innate *aptitude* for them and likewise acting should be *taught* to those who possess the natural gift. No matter the level of the gift, it still needs to be developed, refined and honed through study and practice, practice, practice. *The actor is nothing without the gift, but the gift is nothing without the work.*

TRAINING:

Many actors (I use the term loosely) today are untrained or only partially trained and are grossly unaware of their own ignorance - *mediocrity sees only itself but talent recognizes genius.* Most untrained actors can't scatter horse crap with a two dollar rake, but will sometimes achieve a fine performance by accident, but a trained, scientific actor knows how to <u>*reproduce*</u> the effect over and over again on call. His training will always supply him with the "road map" (BACK STORY) to the effect. Genius will always be an unknown factor, but *technique* will supply the base and the constant to solve the problem. My Father used to say, *"Time and effort will normally take care of ignorance, but stupid is forever".* There is a plethora of actors today who are not sufficiently *gifted* for this trade, but a trained, ungifted actor is surely preferable to a gifted one with *no* training at all. *"It is, I believe, safe to say that no actor ever produced a truly great effect in acting <u>except</u> as a result of long study, close thought, deliberate purpose and <u>careful preparation</u>".* [34]

---

[34] David Belasco, *The Theatre Througyh Its Stage Door, Edited by Louis V. Defoe, New York: Benjamin Blom, 1969.*

NOTES

CHAPTER 12 - AUDITIONING

Auditioning is a paradox in itself. I have preached numerous times in this book, to *"play the moment"*, however, during the process of auditioning, it is virtually impossible. Let's look at the situation; first, in order to "get the part" you must audition for it - unless you are related to someone. Auditioning *normally* involves "reading" first with the casting director alone; sometimes, however, you luck out and get to audition with another actor, but in the norm you read with the casting director who, and I haven't figured this out in my twenty-eight years, normally gives you *nothing* - they just *read* the other lines. Now, whether it is because most CD's are not actors or haven't been actors and have no training in acting skills or they give you nothing on purpose so they can see what you can do on your own, I don't know; it still makes no sense. You just have to roll with the flow.

THE BUBBLE:

Actors are trained, or should be, to play the moment as I have said, and yet in that most important of areas, the *AUDITION*, have to play within themselves if they are to earn the job. I sometimes feel like it is peeing up a well rope. The current auditioning process is, in my opinion, inherently flawed; it is the only time you will *ever* have to perform this way. The only solution is to *"create the bubble"* and create *your own* "moment". I have heard some casting directors say they don't *give* anything because they want to see what you can do; that's like watching someone play baseball to see how well they can ride a horse, but it's their ball game and you have to play by their rules. The important thing is to *get the job*, then you can create a delineated BACK STORY, develop your character so you <u>can</u> *play the moment.*

NOTES

BENJI:

In the event, as I mentioned above, you are lucky enough to audition with another actor, assuming he is trained, you can really reach out and go for it. I auditioned for Joe Camp, the director and creator of "Benji", a few years ago for the CBS *Benji* series (episode - *Ghost Town*). He specifically had all the actors audition in pairs for guest starring spots as a couple of ne'er-do-well, dumb and dumber brothers. I auditioned with an actor whom I had never met before, and luckily, we were of the same level and found an immediate chemistry. During the scene, we both played that chemistry and the timing that comes with it, really got into it, slightly changed some of the dialogue (with permission) and Joe literally fell out of his chair laughing. Needless to say we both were hired for our respective roles - I was the "dumb" brother he was the "dumber". It is fairly rare for actors auditioning together to both get hired, this was the first of two times it has happened to me. However, auditioning with another actor does, in my opinion, greatly enhance your chances of getting the job because you can actually utilize the skills you have worked so hard to acquire. I personally think the current casting process is next to being useless. As an actor and producer, I think the selection process would be far superior if (1) actors are selected first from headshots/resumes; then (2) hold personal interviews; (3) those that survive the interview *perform* a scene with another actor (similar to the old screen test). In this manner the true talent and skills will rise to the surface.

NOTES

RESPONSIBILITY TO THE STORY:

In any case, following the System will stand you in good stead because your first responsibility is *always* to the ***story***. You know (or should) both (all) character's dialogue and will have done preliminary BACK STORIES on them. You should have access (according to SAG rules) to your *"sides"* at least twenty-four hours in advance of your audition. Take that time to *know* the story and do a preliminary BACK STORY for the characters, including their relationship *(Joint Back Story),* even if you have to create it from whole cloth.

COMMITMENT:

Just be sure that you are *"committed"* to the character you create; the worst thing you can do is to play your character on eggshells. I have never played a role that turned out, in the actual production, to be the same as the way they wanted it in the audition. If the casting director gives you direction that you feel is contrary to your concept, you have to go ahead and take it, it won't matter as long as you get the job because the *Director* is the one that counts. Many casting directors think they know the way;... but they can't drive the car. And some casting directors give, what you may feel as, unjustified direction just to see if you can *take* direction; they are just doing their jobs. Keep in mind the cardinal rule of auditioning, no matter what the auditioner says or directs you to do, *NEVER BREAK CHARACTER. "The best actors never let the wheels show."* - Henry Fonda

NOTES

PREPARATION:

Your *responsibility* is to know the story, create your character and learn the dialogue - be prepared, be ready to change on the spot, carve nothing in stone. After acquiring the script material, begin learning the *story* by reading it aloud as an observer, *slowly* with maximum *visualization* (as one would read Kipling) as many times as is possible; *paying no more attention to one character over another.* You are *not* a participant at this point, you are only an *observer.*

THREE SENSES:

The act of reading aloud uses three senses - sight, hearing and *imagery*. Each *successive* reading will enhance your visualization and with it your emotional understanding. Be on your feet and moving, let your *energy* work for you. Somehow physical activity (for most people) is conducive to thinking, at least if the activity calls for no particular attention, like walking. Again, do not focus or pay attention to one character over another, just *concentrate on the story.* You are *not* a participant, you are an observer, a third party, a fly on the wall. You don't like *any* of the characters, they are either very vile and mean or goody-two-shoes sickeningly sweet; make them *caricatures* and take them to a ludicrous level. See, hear, smell, taste and feel everything, *visualize*, *visualize* - create *detailed* pictures in your mind. Wherever the scene takes place, inside, outside; you must create *everything* about your environment in your mind, in detail. Be there.

NOTES

OUT LOUD:

Put the script down and tell yourself, as a third person, an observer, *the story*, what was going on in the scene; be a *gossip*, take it to a ludicrous level, remember, you don't like any of the characters. *You were there*, you saw and heard it all. Focus on the *sequence of events*, all stories have a sequence of events. Only one thing happened first, one thing happened second, etc. Keep repeating the story out loud until *all* events and points of information are clear and in the *order* in which they occurred. When you can tell yourself the story smoothly, with color and in order, move on to your character, your second responsibility.

FULL OF YOUR CHARACTER:

Do your research, then create a preliminary BACK STORY, (you will do a complete BACK STORY when you get the part, an audition BACK STORY is basically an outline) for your character and a shorter BACK STORY for the other character. Be imaginative and creative in your character, make him unique, not a "fence post". Be *full* of your *character*, not *full of yourself.* The further from your own ego the better.

LINES ARE LAST:

Many actors make the mistake of trying to learn their lines before they create their character; that's like putting shoes on a horse *before* you trim his hooves. *Lines are last, always last*. Remember; *Story*, *Research*, *Back Story* and then *Dialogue*.

NOTES

NOW THE LINES:

Now, the lines. You will find that by correctly performing the above, that you *already know most of the dialogue*, you certainly know the *story* and the *story is the basis of all dialogue*.

First divide the scene into French scenes or natural breaks. A French scene is the entrance or exit of *any* energy or life force, a person, an animal, a phone call, an off stage voice, thunder, etc. A natural break can be anywhere; pretend you are a station program director and find spots where you would cut to a commercial; at the end of a question, a look or a specific action. The more breaks or French scenes you can make, the easier it is to learn. Break each French scene or natural break into three equal parts; beginning, middle and end. This is done to help the mind absorb the information faster.

The mind learns from the top down and the bottom up, so the more tops and bottoms you can create, the easier it is for the mind to retrieve the middles. Begin, of course, with the first section; highlight or underline *only* the *important words - to you -* in *each* line of dialogue *(for <u>all</u> characters)*. These words are the ideas or thoughts (events) of the lines, *focus on them only*; it's the *"important"* or *<u>"power"</u>* words where the *emotional context* lies.

SEQUENCING THOUGHTS:

Sequence these thoughts in order of occurrence by writing on a separate page, each line of dialogue. Write *only* the highlighted or underlined words, all other words put "dashes" that are the approximate length of the words they are representing. *(See Fig. 12B) Work only one section at a time.*

NOTES

After you have written each line of dialogue with the highlighted/underlined words and dashes; turn the real script over and read *aloud* from your written page, letting your *mind* fill in the dashes as you read. You should be able to "fill in" 95 to 100% of the dashes on the first read through. Continue rereading the page until you can fill in all dashes correctly and *without* hesitation. Then turn the that page over; you will find that you, in fact, "know" *all* the dialogue. Work with each section until the sequence is clear. This is how you address any situation; you break it down into pieces and address each piece separately. Divide and conquer.

PRACTICE:

With ***practic***e, this entire process should take less than ten minutes per page of dialogue; it will become automatic. Remember this order; *learn and know the story, create your character, then learn your lines. Be COMMITTED.*

Scene from THE NATIONS

EXT. MOLLY ALLGOOD'S HORSE RANCH - DAY

It is a modest but very neatly kept place consisting of THE MAIN HOUSE, BARN, OUTHOUSES, BUNKHOUSE AND CORRALS. In the distance a couple of RANCH HANDS can be seen working with some horses in a BREAKING PEN. Molly is hoeing some weeds from her wheel chair near the front steps. Built on the edge of the porch near the steps is a SEESAW IKE RAMP, to which is attached several graduated gear wheels and a crank. With the use of it, she can roll her chair onto the lower end of the ramp, then crank that end up till the ramp is level, then simply roll the chair onto the

porch. Molly has just finished hoeing the weeds and is on the ramp about to crank it up, when Nellie Ruth enters from the house, drying her hands on an APRON.

NELLIE RUTH

I declare, that contraption never ceases to amaze me!

MOLLY

Right clever, ain't it! Reckon I got my inventiveness from my Pappy. He was always dreamin' up some newfangled doodad... like my convenience. Sure beats those two-holers in town that are a pure source of consternation for someone in my situation.

NELLIE RUTH

Molly, you are truly a remarkable woman.

Molly rolls off the ramp onto the porch.

MOLLY

Ain't I though?

______________________________________ **BREAK**

Nellie Ruth opens the front door for her and she starts rolling in.

MOLLY

You know, child, all that life demands from a body is a little gumption and a willingness to spill some sweat.

INT. MOLLY'S RANCH HOUSE - DAY

Nellie Ruth follows Molly into the kitchen as they talk.

NELLIE RUTH

I guess so. But if I was in a wheelchair, ...
I don't know if I could deal with it.
(beat)
'Course, if it was the Lord's will that I should...

MOLLY

Aw, Lord's will, my fanny! Folks blame the Lord for ever'thin'. Wasn't the Lord's fault I got crippled. It was that tom-fool husband of mine... God rest his soul.

Molly rolls up to the stove and reaches for a steaming COFFEE POT, pouring some into a GRANITE-WARE CUP on the table.

MOLLY

When it come to horses, Walter Allgood didn't know beans from barley. And speakin' of beans, hand me that jar from the cupboard.

BREAK

Nellie Ruth obeys her, then sets a PAN AND COLANDER beside the bean jar. Molly uncaps the jar and pours some of the beans into the pan, begins sorting them, as she talks.

MOLLY

That day before we started to town in the buggy, I warned Walt about that blamed skittish mare... but he wouldn't listen. Oh, how he loved that animal! She was a high stepper and he liked to show her off.

Molly pauses a moment to examine a handful of beans before dropping them in the colander.

NELLIE RUTH

What happened?

MOLLY

Oh... well, we was nearin' the bridge over Crawford's creek...

Molly and Nellie Ruth hear the SOUND OF A HORSE GALLOPING up and a man SHOUTING, interrupting her. The man is SKY, a young Indian who works for Molly. Molly sets aside her work.

______________________________ **FRENCH SCENE**

SKY (O. C.)

Miz Allgood! Miz Allgood! It gonna happen! It gonna happen!

MOLLY

What in tarnation!

Molly spins toward the door fast, Nellie Ruth coming up behind to push.

NELLIE RUTH

_ declare, ___ contraption ____ ceases_ amaze __!

MOLLY

____ clever, ___ _! _____ I ___ __
inventiveness ____ __ Pappy. He ___
_____ dreamin' __ ___ newfangled
_______... ___ __ convenience. ____
beats ____ two-holers __ town ___ __
_ ___ source __ consternation __ someone
_ __ situation.

NELLIE RUTH

Molly, __ __ ___ _ remarkable woman.

MOLLY

Ain't _ though?

Nellie Ruth opens the front door for her and she starts rolling in.

____ BREAK

MOLLY (Cont.)

__ know, child, __ ___ life ______
___ _ body __ _ ___ gumption __ _
willingness _ spill ___ sweat.

NELLIE RUTH

_ guess __. ___ __ I ___ __ _ wheelchair, ...
I ___ know __ _ _____ deal ___ it.
(beat)
'Course, __ __ ___ ___ Lord's __ ___ _
Should...

MOLLY

__, Lord's will, __ fanny! ___ blame
__ Lord __ ever'thin'. ____ __ Lord's
____ I __ crippled. _ __ ___ tom-fool
husband _ mine... God ___ __ soul.

Molly rolls up to the stove and reaches for a steaming COFFEE POT, pouring some into a GRANITE-WARE CUP on the table.

MOLLY (Cont.)

___ it ____ _ horses, Walter Allgood
____ ____ beans ____ barley. __ speaking
_ beans, hand __ ___ jar ___ __ cupboard.

Nellie Ruth obeys her, then sets a PAN AND COLANDER beside the bean jar. Molly uncaps the jar and pours some of the beans into the pan, begins sorting them, as she talks.

____ BREAK

MOLLY (cont.)

___ day _____ __ started __ town __ ___
buggy, _ warned ___ about ___ blamed
_____ mare... __ he _____ listen.
__, how __ loved ___ animal! She __ _
high stepper __ he ____ _ show __ off.

NELLIE RUTH

___ happened?

MOLLY

__... ___, we __ nearin' __ bridge
___ Crawford's ____...

Molly and Nellie Ruth hear the SOUND OF A HORSE GALLOPING up and a man SHOUTING, interrupting her. The man is SKY, a young Indian who works for Molly. Molly sets aside her work.

____ FRENCH SCENE

SKY (O. C.)

Miz ______! ___ Allgood! It
_____ happen! _ gonna _____!

MOLLY

What _ tarnation!

("The Nations" now available on Amazon in novel form: www.tinyurl.com/thenations1)

FOCUS ON THE STORY:

My young acting friend, Vikas Adam, (Vik graduated from Syracuse University with a degree in Fine Arts) asked me one day to teach him this story/line learning system. I picked out a one page scene he had never seen before and started walking him through it. After ten minutes he looked up at me and said, *"You son of a bitch, I feel like an infomercial... I know all the words!... I have never learned lines this fast in my life."* I said, *"Surprise, surprise, Bubba,... when you change the focus from the "words" to the story, you take all the stress and tension off your mind; you will then be relaxed and the "words" will just be there";* the biggest problem most actors have, and it is of their own creation, is they get overwhelmed with all the words. *"Oh, God, I have to know all these words by tomorrow."* When, in reality, by focusing on the story, the dialogue comes into your mind through the back door and you don't even realize it. But it does take some practice, ten minutes... is not acceptable. It's easier to "see" (visualize) the story than it is to "see" the words.

NOTES

TELL THE STORY:

Now that you know the words, *forget them* and just *tell the story*. Remember your studies on Emotionology, tell the story with variety, power visualization and with colors. Acting without emotions is like an eagle without wings. If you have just one more color on your character's canvas, than the other actors, it just may get you the job. Knowing that most actors neglect and have little knowledge of the emotions, will focus on the words and will probably rely on their own personal limited resources of tainted emotions, will put you at the advantage.

EMOTIONOLOGY:

The study of Emotionology will give you a ready source of *Pure Emotions* for your character which increases his options, mobility, uniqueness and choices. Hard work in studying your art is always rewarded with jobs. The jobs are out there for the prepared. I have heard many actors remark, "He was *'lucky'* to have gotten that part.

LUCK:

I am reminded of the old adage, "Luck is when *preparation* meets *opportunity*". Be COMMITTED to *study* and be COMMITTED to *preparedness*; the opportunities are out there and you will be surprised how "lucky" you become. Every actor will get his chance, it's a pity so few are ready for it.

NOTES

CONSCIOUS CONTACT:

. *Acting is a constant, never ending, learning process.* We will forget what we are *taught*, but we will always remember what we have *learned* and we learn by doing. You must have *conscious contact* with what you have been taught through *practice* it to make it learned. We know *about* what we are taught, but we *know* what we have learned. It's like knowing about God and knowing God. *"Learning is not the filling of a pail, but the lighting of a fire.* - William Butler Yeats. *"The solution to all your problems, lies within yourself."* - Anonymous

"It is not the word or expression, but the spaces between that makes it acting."
-KF-

NOTES

CHAPTER 13 - THE FIVE STEPS OF THE PAG SYSTEM

STEP 1. Read the script **slowly** (out loud) with power **visualization** enough times so that the ***story*** is completely imbedded in your mind and your understanding is complete. *(Dramatic interpretation is a result, not a cause. For the actor who truly* ***knows*** *the story,* ***interpretation takes care of itself****.)* Check the individual scenes for French scenes and natural breaks, French scenes occur with each entrance or exit of an energy or life force. Lines are learned by FRENCH SCENES, NATURAL BREAKS and VISUALIZATION .

STEP 2. CONTENT - POINTS OF INFORMATION. Apply these rules throughout the rest of this process.

a. Read the words **ALOUD. CONCENTRATE ON THE *STORY AS AN OBSERVER!***

b. Use as many of the senses as possible, especially ***imagery*.**

c. **BOOK DOWN!!!** Do not hold the script after five read throughs.

d. Take all Characters to **Caricature** - You don't like any of them. They are either sickeningly sweet, or terribly bad.

e. You are responsible for **all Dialogue.** Do not pay any more attention to one character than another. Just pay attention to and focus on the **story.**

f. Assume that you know ***Everything*** about the characters. You know what they know. ***Anything*** they know, you know.

g. Be on your Feet and moving. Make your energy work for you. Somehow, physical activity is conducive to thinking, at least if the activity calls for no particular attention, like walking.

NOTES

h. You are the ***THIRD PERSON - A GOSSIP, AN OBSERVER.*** You are ***NOT*** a participant or a character!

i. See and Hear **everything.** ***VISUALIZE - CREATE PICTURES IN YOUR MIND.*** **FOCUS ON THE STORY.**

j. ***THINK THE THOUGHTS, SEE THE PICTURES, SPEAK THE WORDS***.

k. Just ***have a HOOT!***

Walk away from the script and, as the observer, tell YOURSELF, **out loud**, the story,... what was going on in the scene. Mention all points of information **in order**. Don't forget to **visualize.** Remember: ***YOU WERE THERE!***

REPEAT STEP 2. UNTIL ALL INFORMATION POINTS AND THE **STORY** ARE **CLEAR.**

STEP 3. THE BACK STORY.

CREATE A *BACK STORY* FOR ALL CHARACTERS, (The back story for your character will be **highly detailed**, the other characters will be abbreviated and be seen from your character's eyes) **A BACK STORY IS A COMPLETE LIFE HISTORY AND AN IN-DEPTH PSYCHOLOGICAL PROFILE OF THE CHARACTERS** in writing, IN OTHER WORDS, WHAT MAKES THEM TICK AND **WHY?** (BACK STORIES dictate what **choices** they will make.) There are three elements of characterization, ALL OF WHICH YOU **CREATE** FROM YOUR **BACK STORY**, BEGINNING WITH THE ***GIVEN CIRCUMSTANCES*** (from the writer and from you):

a. **INTERNAL** (Becoming familiar with inner mechanisms)

(1) His background and personality. (Which you **create**)

NOTES

(2) Memories: (Physical, Emotional, Knowledge, and Anticipation of future events the character is anticipating or dreading)

(The quality of life the character lives has an effect upon his internal Characterizations.)

b. **EXTERNAL**

(1) External characterizations are an outgrowth of INTERNAL, dictating the way the person dresses, walks, talks, looks at others, listens to others, expresses ideas, copes with conflict or crisis and shows love. *As within, so without*. If you don't go within, you go without.

(2) All physical movements should reflect the INTERNAL and should be distinct, **subtle** and **imaginative.** *As within, so without.*

(REMEMBER, NO MATTER WHAT CHARACTER YOU CREATE; *IT IS NOT YOU*. IT IS AN *ASSUMED FANTASY PERSONALITY*)

c. **TRANSFORMATIONS**

(1) Transformation into the character demands discipline.

(2) Transformation must be nourished by the other elements.

(3) Gathering & selecting the internal & external details of the **BACK STORY** provides the material for transformation into the character. Your **BACK STORY** will dictate what **choices** your character will make. Avoid choreographing choices, trust the instincts and impulses of the *character*. The character's actions will always flow from the character traits you established in the Back Story.

NOTES

(4) **Study** and chart the **emotions**. The character **you create in your BACK STORY** will express himself differently than you. He is **not you**, he will react differently to situations than **you.**

ACTING WITHOUT EMOTIONS IS LIKE AN EAGLE WITHOUT WINGS

***Do not use your own emotional memories*, use fantasy memories, create Physical, Emotional, Knowledge memories and Future anticipation of events of the character. Play the moment and visualize the causes (stimuli) of the emotions of the character from the BACK STORY at that point in time.**

The actors job is to ABSORB these details and use them naturally *as* (not like) the character (outpicture).

DO NOT GO TO STEP 4 UNTIL YOU HAVE BACK STORIED YOUR CHARACTER!!

STEP 4. LEARN THE DIALOGUE - SEQUENCE OF EVENTS (See Fig. 12A & 12B)

The **story** only happened one way. Only one thing happened **first**, then one thing happened **second**, etc. Break each scene into French scenes or Natural breaks and break those into 3 equal parts:

NOTES

BEGINNING, MIDDLE, and END. This is done to help the brain absorb the information faster. The brain retrieves top down and bottom up. By making more tops and more bottoms, it is easier for the mind to retrieve the middles. Highlight or underline **only** the **IMPORTANT WORDS (TO YOU)** in **each** line of dialogue (for ALL characters). These words are the **IDEAS** or thoughts ***(events)*** of the line, **focus on them only**. **Sequence** these thoughts in order of occurrence by writing on a separate page each line of dialogue. **Write only the underlined/highlighted words, all other words put "dashes"** (the dashes should be the approximate length of the words they are replacing). Work only one section at a time. Then read **aloud** from the page you have just written (but focus on the story), filling in the "dashes" orally without looking at the copy. You should be able to fill in 95 to 100% of the dashes. Continue rereading the page until you can fill in all dashes correctly and without hesitation. Then turn the page over, you will find that you probably will know all the dialogue. You will work with each section (beginning, middle and end) ***separately*** until the sequence of events is clear. Divide and conquer.

STEP 5. THE PAG LINE LEARNING TEST

Purpose: To insure that you know all the thoughts **without** having to **think** about them. Ask someone to read **ANY** thought of dialogue out of sequence so that you can give the following thought. When you can give every thought ***OUT OF SEQUENCE,*** you are ready to move on to rehearsal, let your juices flow and play the moment.

WITH PRACTICE!!!, THIS ENTIRE PROCESS SHOULD TAKE LESS THAN 10 MINUTES PER PAGE OF DIALOGUE

NOTES

We can shape clay into a pot, but it is the emptiness inside that holds whatever we want.
- Lao Tzu -

THE THREE MOST VITAL ELEMENTS FOR AN ACTOR ARE:

PASSION, KNOWING THE STORY AND CREATING A DETAILED AND COMPREHENSIVE BACK STORY!!

YOU MUST SEE THE CHARACTER BEFORE YOU CAN BE THE CHARACTER!

DON'T THINK ABOUT IT, JUST DO IT!!!

THE PAG SYSTEM© IS BECOMING THE PARADIGM OF THE NEW AGE ACTOR!

GOOD ACTING IS AN OASIS IN THE HEART THAT WILL NEVER BE REACHED BY THE CARAVAN OF THINKING.
Paraphrased from *GIBRAN*

If the Heart is empty,
then what's in the Head doesn't matter.
- KF

NOTES

CHAPTER 14 - THE PERFORMANCE

THE DESTINATION:

Preparation is the journey; the *performance* is the destination. The performance is far and away the easiest and most fun part of acting, *if* you have done your preparation. We have done all the *hard* work in preparation; learned the story, researched, written our BACK STORY and *created* our character, learned the dialogue, gone through the horrendous auditioning process and gotten the job. But in reality, the *"job"* was the preparation; the *"reward"* is the performance. So, for God's sake, don't drop the ball now.

You will never "drop the ball" if you have *properly* gone through the preparation process. I know it sounds like I am beating this preparation thing to death, but without it, even if you got hired because you fit perfectly the preconceived image the director had for the character or your brother-in-law is the producer, you now must *perform*.

TRUST YOUR PREPARATION:

No one can tell you or teach you *how* to perform. That is something you have to trust the character you have *created* to do and trust the *preparation* behind the character. I refer back to the quotation I made in Chapter 10 by Sir Laurence Olivier; *"If you're practiced, rehearsed and thoroughly versed (know the story), you have something to offer. You know what the lines are about, but you haven't waited for the final, ultimate way of saying them or handling a single moment... take care of the play (story) and let genius take care of itself". "Spectacular achievement is always preceded by unspectacular preparation". - Roger Staubach*

NOTES

IMAGES:

Surround yourself with images. Ethel Boileau wrote, *"You will see images as in a vision mirrored in your imagination. You will give them form, substance and reality, but you will never know quite whence they come. They are greater than yourself - they will have a life of their own which is not your life - a mind which is not the reflection of your own."* You must see the character before you can be the character and the character must see what he says. *"Actions are words moving. Words are thoughts expressed. Thoughts are ideas formed. Ideas are energies come together. Energies are forces released."*[35] -Neale Donald Walsch

Once you *free yourself* from the ever present pressure of your own intellectualized *personal* (ego) interference with the creative process, you will enter the sphere of *inspiration* that lies beyond the intellect. *"The better the actor, the more completely is he able to eliminate the personal equation." - John Barrymore*

EXPERIENCE:

Performing requires practice. Just like professional football players, you have to get as many *"snaps"* as possible and also like *all* athletes, it is *experience* that is the best teacher. One movie is worth a year in the classroom. Whether it is doing "Little Theatre", a Commercial, a TV show or Movie, there is no substitute for actually doing it in front of a paying audience or a camera when your butt is on the line. No coach, teacher or class can give you that kind of experience; you have to *earn* it. *"In theory, there is no difference between theory and practice. In practice, there is."* - Yogi Berra

---

[35] Ibid

NOTES

PLAY THE MOMENT:

I don't know who originally came up with the phrase, *"Play the moment"*. Checkov referred to it as *"constant improvisation"*. I don't care what you call it but you must trust the instincts of your *character* and allow him to react to whatever is going on in the scene and *tell the story.* Don't think about it, don't analyze it, just lend your character your equipment and then *"get the hell out of the way"* and let your character *"play the moment"*. You know the lines, but your character doesn't, leave him alone and let the audience or the camera *see* the thought processes that creates his dialogue or action. Jessica Lange has said; *"The worst thing an actor can do is to determine the outcome of the scene before you do it."* Remember, always play to the audience or camera. They can't see your character *think* if he does not *favor* his audience/camera. You may feel, in your observation of your creation, that your character *cut one hell of a hog* with some inspirational thought process, but if the camera/audience didn't catch it, you've got diddly squat.

DON'T NEGATE IMPULSES:

Take care that <u>*your mouth and eyes match*</u> and don't choreograph pauses unless they are part of the *"given circumstances"* from the writer. Let the *"pauses"* come naturally to your character, don't negate *his* impulses. Your character *knows* the story; *leave him alone, get out of the way and let him tell it, "genius <u>will</u> take care of itself."* It is the silence between the words that makes great acting/storytelling just as it is the silence between the notes that makes the music. *Shake the dialogue until all the words fall away; what is left is the art of true acting.*

NOTES

I wrote this book for all the *committed* and *dedicated* actors who are constantly seeking to improve their craft, their art, in the hope that it opens their mind to a measure of curiosity of another way to strive to reach the pinnacle of acting, and hopefully even a small hint of gratitude; then this book will have served what I hoped to present. The PAG System© is not a "silver bullet" or panacea, it will not cure all the ills of acting, nor will it instantly make you a better actor just by the act of reading it; that requires study, practice and work; actors learn by *doing*. Neither I nor anyone else can teach you how to perform, that is acquired through experience and from whatever level of talent you were given, I can only hope to teach you how to prepare. If *talent* is the horse, then surely experience/training is the jockey. Acting is more feelings and instincts than rules. Be on time, know the story and don't run into the furniture.

KEN FARMER

WISDOM GROWS IN DIRECT RATIO TO ONE'S AWARENESS OF HIS OWN IGNORANCE.
-KF-

"THE QUALITY OF A PERSON'S LIFE IS IN DIRECT PROPORTION TO THEIR COMMITMENT TO EXCELLENCE, REGARDLESS OF THEIR CHOSEN FIELD OF ENDEAVOR".
-VINCE LOMBARDI-

NOTES

CHAPTER 15 - EXERCISES, FINDING YOUR CENTER:

The actor must find and activate his energy centers. These centers are referred to as "CHAKRAS" and must be activated in each person in order to develop and enhance "focus" and "concentration".

First, the actor must isolate the main center:

Lie on the floor (you will eventually be able to do this sitting in a chair or even standing); close your eyes and create a visualization of a "golden light" eminating from inside of you, this is your master center. This golden light shines or works through the seven energy centers or *"power points"*. The clearer and sharper your visualization of this golden light, the easier it is for you to access and release energy from it. This master center is where all stimuli or causal factors are received which triggers responses of emotion, thought, voice and movement - your equipment.

As mentioned above, there are seven energy centers in the body corresponding with aspects of your emotional, mental and physical expression (outflow). It is vital that these centers be activated, active and operating for the actor if he is to absorb, visualize and express his creation (character).

A. The RED Center:

Is the root center; your source of maximum energy. It is located in your pelvic region. While lying on your back, after activating the master center, visualize a RED BALL floating above your pelvic region (the sexual area), it is responsible for the physical life force; sexuality; reaction to the moment;

spontaneity; instinct; survival; vitality, power and energy. Continually sharpen the image in your mind until it is crystal clear; then proceed to make the red ball grow larger. This will take practice. Make it grow larger, until it is as large as a beach ball, then compress it back down to the size of a baseball and absorb it back into the body. You will probably only get a small, fuzzy, transparent cloud on your first efforts, but as above, it takes practice. You will be amazed at the clarity and control you will achieve in about two weeks. I have had several students with ADD (Attention Deficit Disorder) who were on medication, that were able to stop taking it after a few weeks of this exercise.

B. The ORANGE Center:

Is the spleen center; between the pubis and navel. This center controls; instinctive feelings (automatic reaction patterns); depth; well-being health; will; self-confidence. After you have brought the RED BALL back into your body; create the ORANGE BALL over the region between the pubis and navel and go through the same procedure as above.

C. The YELLOW Center:

Is the solar plexus center. This center controls; the diaphragm, vulnerability; resistance, courage; wisdom; and intuition. Same as above; remember crystal clear imagery, see even the texture of the ball.

D. The GREEN Center:

Is the heart center; center of the chest. This center controls; air, touch; love; compassion; harmony; security; self-assertion; serenity; warmth. Same as above.

E. The BLUE Center:

Is the throat center, controlling communication; inspiration spirituality; truth; loyalty; self-expression. Same as above.

F. The INDIGO Center:

Is the brow or forehead center, controlling the imagination; thought; creativity; ideas; insight; fantasy life; perception; dreams; intelligence and wit. Same as above.

G. The WHITE Center:

Is the crown or top of the head, controlling Talent; transformation; intelligence, freedom and bliss. Same as above. Continuing to use your imagery; after you have reached the WHITE Center, channel and split the WHITE BALL into two columns, or pillars of white fire; as if you had two rocket ships with their noses down instead of up and are shooting the white flames from their engines straight up, side by side. When this image eventually becomes clear, begin arcing the tips of the columns of white fire toward each other until they just touch. Hold them there a few moments and then return them back to the starting point. This ends the sequence of the exercise of color meditation and focus.

RED, ORANGE and YELLOW are the warm, energy creating colors for the body and the emotions. BLUE, INDIGO and WHITE are the cool and more imaginative colors. GREEN is balance, the marriage of the warm and cool. As I am sure you know, yellow and blue combined, create green. RED is the BODY; YELLOW the MIND; BLUE the SPIRIT. These are the primary colors.

Some of the imagery you create will affect you more or less than others; the point being, that you create a time and space to find, actuate and develop your powers of concentration, visualization, ability to focus and relaxation. You may notice that you cannot get all the color balls to the same size; this means you are not in balance and must work harder on the areas in which you are weakest. Eventually, with practice, all the color balls will become equal. You will, in all likelihood, create your own imagery and symbols after a time. This exercise is a guide to allow you to find your own way.

DEVELOPING THE IMAGINATION:

There are literally thousands of exercises to help the actor develop his imagination. Below are just a few to get you started.

THE WALL:

Visualize a stone wall, a stone wall made of irregular native rock. See the shapes, the colors, feel the texture. Take it apart, stone by stone and then rebuild it.

THE ROOM:

Create a well furnished and appointed room for one of your characters; furniture, rugs, pictures, wall paper, draperies, knickknacks (dust catchers), books, magazines, vases (with flowers), a cat or dog, view, light fixtures, etc. Now that you have created this well lived in room,... rearrange it, piece by piece. Then list 30 items in the room that have special meaning to the character; keepsake, photo, favorite sweater, souvenir, lucky charm, old tennies, etc.

THE LIBRARY:

Create a library, (large or small) filled with all sorts of books, floor to ceiling. See the titles, the colors, size, textures and smells of the books, the reading tables and chairs. Now hit it with an earthquake; all the books in the floor; put them back.

THE PICTURE:

Pick a picture. It can be a masterpiece or any picture, preferably a picture of a person, say the MADONNA. Age her in your mind's eye (sort of like the picture of DORIAN GREY), to an old woman; gray hair, wrinkles, drooping jowls, etc., then bring her back all the way to infancy.

THE FOREST:

Find a picture of a forest. Then, with imagery, go inside the forest to see the individual trees, the birds, animals, shrubs, streams, etc. Make a list and write your descriptions down. Should be at least thirty to fifty items.

THE ALBUM:

Create a picture album for a character in your mind. See at least thirty photographs involving the character; write down the description of each photo in detail. Who is with the character; what are they doing; what is the setting; is it color or black and white; how is everyone dressed; what season is it, etc.

THE IMPROV:

Take the list of photographs above in the "ALBUM" and do a short, three minute improvisation of each photograph.

THE PENCIL:

Take a pencil, throw it on the floor; then figure out *thirty* different ways to find and pick up the pencil.

THE MIRROR:

Go to the Dictionary of Emotions; pick a primary emotion with at least 10 secondary emotions to begin with. Study them all; then go to a mirror and do all the emotions with only subtle facial expressions (no dialogue). Concentrate on the eyes. Think the thought, see the imagery of the emotion. This exercise is good for at least a year or two, considering there are almost 900 emotions in your book. The next step or exercise is to add body language to each emotion. It works even better if you do this exercise with a friend or partner and read each emotion to each other, allowing only three seconds per emotion. Remember, no vocalizations.

THE JUMP EMOTION IMPROV: (Viola Spolin)

This is another exercise that requires a friend or partner or coach. Each of you picks a two to three minute monologue; have pre prepared 3x5 "flash cards" (at least 8 to 10) with a different emotion boldly written on each. One of you begins performing his monologue; the other will snap his fingers every ten to twenty seconds and hold up a different "flash card". You must *instantly* change to whatever emotion is written on the card, no matter where you are in the monologue, don't hold back. The "flash card" emotion may be diametrically opposite to the emotion your character is feeling at the particular point in the monologue; go with it. When you have finished the monologue doing the "jump emotion improv"; *immediately* do the monologue again without the "flash cards". You should find that the character will reach a greater, much more open, depth of storytelling. (Can also be done with scene dialogue.)

STOP AND GO: (Jeremy Whelan)

"The Stop and Go" is one of the best exercises I have ever seen to centralize or sharpen focus on the *"moment"*. You will see some very significant byproducts in the depth of the emotional outpicturing of a scene. This exercise works best with a partner, in class or rehearsal. You should have already gone through the five steps of The Pag System©; the story, character and lines should be well in hand and you are ready to rehearse. Stop and Go is performed thusly; while rehearsing the scene, your partner and you will swap control. (Unless you are in class, then another class member or the instructor will exercise control.) While your partner is doing a line, find an emotional point and *"snap"* your fingers. Your partner must *stop dialogue* (don't freeze), but *both of you stay in the moment, continuing physical activity*, focusing on the *emotion* until you snap your fingers again. You can *"hold"* this moment up to a couple of minutes; but don't initially, until you get the feel of the technique. It can get a little hairy. Alternate turns until the scene is finished. Then run the scene straight, I think you will be pleasantly surprised at the results. You'll find creativity and emotional depth you didn't know existed. It gets to be a hoot.

THE COSTUME:

Pick any *character* and create 10 (ten) different costumes for that character; evening, business, home, casual, sport, church, etc. Write *complete* descriptions of each outfit down to the underclothing (if any); include color choices, favorite styles and type of material(s) that the *character* prefers. List and describe what is in his or her pocket, purse and/or wallet, include photos of family, friends, pets, places, etc. If your character is of a *"period"*, be sure to research that period for style, etc.

Using the above exercises a guides, see how many additional exercises *you* can create. Exercises should be done *daily*. Always begin with the "Chakras", for focus, visualization, concentration and relaxation. To be able to *Visualize with Power,* you must practice daily.

"YOU CAN GET BY ON CHARM, WIT, GRIT AND BULL SHIT FOR ABOUT FIFTEEN MINUTES, AFTER THAT YOU'D BETTER KNOW SOMETHING".
KF

CREDIT AND THANKS ARE ACKNOWLEDGED TO:

Peter Brown:
Cliff Osmond:
Gene Hackman:
James Caan:
Alan Alda:
Jack Lemmon:
Jessica Lange:
Robert Altman:
Meryl Streep:
Whoopi Goldberg:
Michael Cain:
Kevin Spacey:
Master Yoda:
Bob Weatherford, “The Weatherford Instant Line Learning Technique”:
Macdara Mac Uibh Aille:
Eryn Brooke:
Britt McEachern:
Denton Blane Everett:
Sir Laurence Olivier, "On Acting": "Great Acting":
John Barrymore, "From Comedy to Tragedy; an Interview with John Barrymore"
By Helen Ten Broeck, "Theatre Magazine":
Charlotte Crocker, Victor A. Fields and Will Broomall, “Taking The Stage”:
William Hooker Gillette, "The Illusion of the First Time in Acting":
Tom Hanks:
Billy Bob Thornton:
James Cameron:
Mark Kasdan:
David Blasco, "The Theatre Through It's Stage Door":
Ben Johnson:
Robert Reese Farmer:
Gibran: "The Prophet"
Dion Boucault, " The Art of Acting":
Anthony Hopkins:
Patrick Stewart:
Ted Kotcheff:
Konstantin Stanislavski: "Art Notes"
Michael Checkov:
Sanford Meisner:
Joseph Jefferson, "The Autobiography of Joseph Jefferson":

Henry Irving:
Henry Fonda:
Ron Howard:
Noble Willingham:
Rowena Balos: "The Human Instrument":
Neale Donald Walsch, "Conversations with God":
Claude Bernard:
Ethel Boileau:
Johann Wolfgang von Goethe:
Ben Hecht:
William Butler Yeats:
Roger Staubach:
Yogi Berra:
Vikas Adam:
Vince Lombardi:

APPENDIX A

THE PAG SYSTEM©

A DICTIONARY *OF* EMOTIONS

ALL OF THE EMOTIONS ON THE FOLLOWING PAGES, PRIMARY AND SECONDARY, MAY BE PLACED UNDER THE TWO *PRIME* EMOTIONS:

LOVE FEAR

A DICTIONARY OF EMOTIONS

A

PRIME: LOVE

Primary:

ABANDON - A complete surrender to feelings or impulses.

Secondary:

ENTHUSIASM - Great excitement or interest in a subject or cause.

EXUBERANCE - High spirited, lively.

SPONTANEITY - Arising from a momentary impulse.

PRIME: FEAR

ABANDONED - To feel deserted; forsaken

Secondary:.

DESERTED - To leave alone.

FORSAKEN - To be renounced; left alone.

FRIENDLESS - To be without a friend.

JILTED - To be cast off callously.

NEGLECTED - To be ignored.

OUTCAST - Excluded from society.

PRIME: FEAR

ADAMANT - Unshakable; refusing to yield.
AGGRESSIVE - Self assertive; forceful
HEADSTRONG - Very stubborn; bullheaded.
CONTRARY - Willful or perverse; opposite in character.
DETERMINED - To have a firmness of purpose.
INSISTENT - To be firm; to assert or demand.
MULISH - Feeling sullen; stubborn.
RELENTLESS - Unyielding; pitiless; persistent.
RESOLUTE - Unwavering; firm or determined.
RIGID - Fixed; not flexible.
STUBBORN - Unwilling to change; obstinate.
UNCOMPROMISING - Unyielding; stubborn.
WILLFUL - Deliberate, voluntary; obstinate.

PRIME: LOVE

ADMIRE - To regard with pleasure, wonder, to esteem or revere.
ADORE - To worship or regard with deep love.
ESTEEM - To regard with admiration or respect.
HONOR - Respect highly, revere.
IDOLIZE - Adore or love to excess.
RESPECT - To regard with deferential esteem.
REVERE - Hold in deep respect or veneration.
VENERATE - To respect deeply.

PRIME: FEAR

AFRAID - Filled with fear or apprehension.

Secondary:

ANGST - Anxiety, neurotic fear; guilt, remorse.
APPREHENSIVE - Suspicion or fear of future trouble.
AWE - A mixed emotion of respect tinged with fear.
DAUNTED - Intimidated.

DISMAYED - Discouraged or depressed fearfully; dread.
DISTRESSED - To suffer anxiety.
DREAD - Overwhelming apprehension and awe.
FEARFUL - An illusion of anxiety, reverence and dread.
FRIGHTENED - To be suddenly afraid; alarmed.
HESITANT - Slight apprehension.
INTIMIDATED - Filled with fear; overawed, cowed.
PARALYZED - Inoperative with fear; unable to move.
POLTROONERY - State of extreme cowardice.
RECREANT - Cowardly or craven.
TIMOROUS - Subject to fear, timid.
TREPIDATION - Dread, apprehension, anxious.
TERRIFIED - Having extreme fear.
UNSURE - Uncertainty, faltering, irresolute, doubtful.
WARY - Cautious; prudent.

PRIME: FEAR

AGITATED - Excited, troubled, disturbed, discombobulated.

Secondary:

FAZED - Disconcerted.
RUFFLED - Flustered.
UPSET - Emotionally disturbed or agitated.

PRIME: FEAR

ALARMED - Sudden feeling of fear; disturbed, excited.

Secondary:

DISTRESSED - Extreme mental, physical, emotional pain.
FEARFUL - Experiencing fear.
FRIGHTENED - Terrified or scared of something or someone.
HORRIFIED - Painful and intense fear or dismay.
PANIC - Sudden overpowering terror.
PETRIFIED - Paralyzed with terror.
RATTLED - Stirred up, roused, nervous.

ROUSED - Provoked from state of security to excited activity.

SCARED - Filled with fear or terror.

SHAKEN - To tremble with fear or shock; become unstable.

PRIME: FEAR

ANGRY - Feeling of wrath, ire, displeasure, resentment, extreme vexation.

Secondary:

ALIENATED - Unfriendly, estranged.

ASPERITY - Ill temper, harshness, roughness.

BITTER - Grievous, full of affliction.

CROSS - Showing ill humor, annoyed.

DISPLEASED - Unsatisfied, annoyed or irritated.

DISTEMPERED - Disturbed, ill at ease.

ESTRANGED - Unfriendly, hostile.

GOADED - Incited toward some disposition or action.

HARD - Not easily moved; unfeeling, hostile.

HUFFED - A sudden rush of offended dignity.

ILL-HUMORED - Given to bad moods, sullen.

INCITED - Stimulated to a fit of anger.

INSULTED - Having one's self-respect offended.

IRASCIBLE - Easily angered; prone to outbursts of temper.

LIVID - Extremely angry.

MIFFED - Taking offense.

NETTLED - Irritated, vexed, annoyed, upset.

OFFENDED - Wounded in feelings, affronted.

PIQUED - Having one's interest or curiosity aroused.

PISSED - (pissed off) Irritaded, angry.

PROVOKED - Irritated to anger, annoyed.

RESENT - To feel bitter.

RILED - To be made angry, irritated.

SORE - A state of being irritated or resentful.

VEXED - Annoyed, bothered.

PRIME: FEAR

ANNOYED - Bothered or irritated; perturbed.

Secondary:

AGGRAVATED - Provoked, exasperated, displeased.
ANTAGONIZED - Opposed to another by provocation.
BOTHERED - Irked, anxious or concerned.
BUGGED - Pestered.
CHAFED - Irritated.
DISGRUNTLED - Discontented or unsatisfied.
DISPLEASED - Unsatisfied, irritated; to dislike.
EXASPERATED - Frustrated, irritated.
GALLED - Irritated, vexed.
I*RKED* - Disgusted, irritated, bored.
TANTALIZED - Tormented, teased.

PRIME: FEAR

APATHETIC - Uninterested, indifferent, not caring.

Secondary:

BLASÉ - Uninterested, bored.
BORED - Made weary by tedious or dull repetition.
CASUAL - Showing little concern.
DEADENED - Deprived of vitality.
DISINTERESTED - Without concern; indifferent.
DISSOLUTE - Relaxed, lacking firmness of temperament.
EASYGOING - Without worry or concern.
HALFHEARTED - Lacking interest or spirit.
LACKADAISICAL - Lacking spirit or liveliness.
LETHARGIC - Sluggishness, inactivity.
LISTLESS - Lacking energy or enthusiasm.
NONCHALANT - Coolly unconcerned or indifferent.
PASSIVE - No visible reaction or resistance, compliant.
PHLEGMATIC - Calm, stolid temperament.
RELUCTANT - Disinclined.

APATHETIC (Continued)

SHIFTLESS - Lacking ambition or purpose.

SLOTHFUL - Given to lazy or sluggish behavior or moods.

SPIRITLESS - Lacking courage, vigor or animation.

TORPID - Dormant, deprived of the power of motion or feelings.

WITHDRAWN - Emotionally unresponsive, shy.

PRIME: FEAR

AROUSED - Stirred to activity; excitement

Secondary:

AWAKE - Alert.

AWARE - Having knowledge or cognizance; mindful.

DISTURBED - Upset emotionally; disquieted

EXCITED - Roused to stimulated to strong emotion.

HOT - Intensity of emotion; sexually aroused; lustful; indignant.

INSPIRED - Stimulated creatively; noble emotion.

INVIGORATED - Animated, stimulated.

MOVED - Affected by emotion; stirred.

OVEREXCITED - Excessive excitement.

STIMULATED - To rouse to activity or heightened action.

B

PRIME: FEAR

BEWILDERED - Perplexed or confused, mystified; dazed.

Secondary:

ADDLED - To make or become confused.

BEDAZZLED - Dazzled to a point of confusion or amazement.

BOGGLED - Overwhelmed with astonishment.

BENUMBED - Feeling totally stupefied.

CONFOUNDED - Brought into confusion.
CONFUSED - Unclear, addled; lacking logical order.
DAZZLED - Deeply impressed, overwhelmed or amazed.
FUDDLED - A state of confusion.
FLABBERGASTED - Dumbfounded.
LOST - Distraught; gone astray.
MUDDLED - Confused.
STUPOROUS - A state of reduced sensibility; dazed.

PRIME: FEAR

BELLIGERENT - Hostile, eager to fight.

Secondary:

ACERBIC - Bitter and sharp in speech , manner or temper.
ACID - Unpleasant disposition.
ARGUMENTATIVE - Given to arguing; disputatious.
BELLICOSE - Pugnacious; warlike in nature.
CENSORIOUS - Tending to be critical.
CONTENTIOUS - Quarrelsome.
CRUEL - Intentionally causing pain or suffering on others.
CYNICAL - Believing all people are motivated by selfishness.
DISPUTATIOUS - Given to dispute.
INDIGNANT - Feeling angry due to some injustice.
MALIGNING - To speak evil of; to defame.
MALEVOLENT - Exhibiting ill will.
MORDANT - Bitingly sarcastic.
SARDONICLY - Scornfully mocking.
SARCASTIC - Given to cutting, ironic remarks.
SPITEFUL - To be mean or evil toward another.
VENGEFUL - Desiring vengeance.
VINDICTIVE - Vengeful; spiteful.

C

PRIME: LOVE

CHARMED - Attracted to or fascinated with; delighted and pleased.

Secondary:

ABSORBED - Totally mentally concentrated; engrossed.
ALLURED - Enticed by charm or other attraction.
BEGUILED - Misled, diverted; amused or delighted.
BEWITCHED - Enchanted; fascinated or captivated.
CAPTIVATED - Fascinated by something or someone.
DELUDED - To deceived the mind in judgment of.
DIVERTED - Distracted.
ENAMORED - Inflamed with love.
ENRAPTURED - Filled with delight.
ENTICED - Attracted by arousing hope or desire; lure.
ENCHANTED - Bewitched; to attract and delight.
ENTRANCED - Carried away with delight.
ENTHRALLED - Fascinated; enslaved.
FASCINATED - Holding an intense interest or attraction for.
INFATUATED - Inspired with unreasoning love or attachment.
MESMERIZED - Hypnotized.
MARVELING - Filled with wonder or surprise.
RAVISH - To overwhelm with emotion.
SMITTEN - Inflamed with love.
SPELLBOUND - Fascinated as if by a spell.

PRIME: FEAR

CONFUSED - To be unclear in mind or purpose; bewildered.

Secondary:

ABASHED - Disconcerted.
ADDLED - Muddled.

BAFFLED - Frustrated, stymied, thwarted, foiled.

DISCOMBOBULATED - A state of being upset, confused.

DISCONCERTED - Thrown into disarray.

DISTRACTED - Emotionally unsettled; troubled.

DUMBFOUNDED - Filled with astonishment and perplexity.

GROGGY - Unsteady and dazed.

HAZY - Unclear or vague.

PERPLEXED - Puzzled.

PERTURBED - Disturbed, agitated.

PUZZLED - Mentally confused with a difficult problem.

D

PRIME: FEAR

DEPRESSED - Low in spirits; dejected.

Secondary:

ABASHED - Disconcerted.

ATRIBILIOUS - Melancholy.

BLUE - Downhearted or low.

CHEERLESS - Low in spirits; sad.

DAUNTED - Intimidated or discouraged.

DASHED - Daunted; abashed.

DEJECTED - Being low in spirits.

DESPAIR - Complete loss of hope.

DESPONDENCY - Loss of hope; dejection.

DISCOMFORT - Mental or bodily distress.

DISCOURAGED - Being deprived of confidence, hope or spirit.

DISHEARTENED - Having your spirit or resolution destroyed.

DISMAYED - Full of dread or apprehension.

DISPIRITED - Disheartened.

DOWNHEARTED - Low in spirit.

DOWNCAST - Depressed; low in spirits.
FORLORN - Nearly hopeless.
INCONSOLABLE - Forlorn.
LOW - Mentally depressed; sad.
MALAISE - A vague feeling of depression or illness.
MELANCHOLY - Habitually sad.
MIRTHLESS - Absence of gladness and gaiety.
MOPY - Gloomy or dejected.
PENSIVE - Deeply thoughtful.
UNHAPPY - Not happy; discontented.

PRIME: FEAR

DISGUSTED - To feel repelled, averse or offended.

Secondary:

ABHORRENCE - A feeling of repugnance.
AVERSION - Intense dislike.
DISAPPROBATION - Moral disapproval; condemnation.
DISTASTE - Dislike.
DISAPPROVAL - Condemnation or censure.
FED UP - Surfeited, extremely bored or tired.
HORRIFIED - Intensely averse or feeling repugnance.
LOATHE - To dislike greatly; abhor.
NAUSEATED - Feeling of aversion to the point of being ill.
REPUGNANCE - A feeling of aversion.
REPULSED - Rejecting from disgust.
REVOLTED - To be filled with abhorrence.
REVULSION - To turn away with feelings of loathing.

PRIME: FEAR

DOUBTFUL - Feeling uncertain; ambiguous.

Secondary:

AGNOSTIC - Skeptic, without positive proof.
AMBIGUOUS - Uncertain; more than one interpretation.

DUBIOUS - Fraught with uncertainty; undecided; questionable.

HESITATING - Irresolute or undecided.

INDEFINITE - Unclear, undecided.

INCREDULITY - skeptical; disbelieving.

MISGIVING - A feeling of doubt or distrust.

MISTRUST - Suspicion or doubt.

NIHILISM - Extreme skepticism and disbelief.

QUESTIONABLE - Open to doubt.

SKEPTICAL - A questioning attitude.

UNCERTAIN - Not having sure knowledge.

UNSETTLED - Likely to change.

VACILLATING - To swing indecisively.

WARY - Prudent; cautious; on guard.

E

PRIME: LOVE

EMPATHETIC - Identifying with and understanding the feelings of another.

Secondary:

APPRECIATE - Recognizing aesthetic value.

BENEVOLENT - Well-wishing; desirous of good.

CHARITABLE - Tolerant in judging others.

COMPASSIONATE - A deep awareness of the feelings of others.

FEEL - To be aware of; sympathy.

HUMANE - Kind or compassionate; respecting life.

SYMPATHETIC - Expressing feelings for; favorably inclined.

UNDERSTANDING - Empathize with the feelings of another.

F

PRIME: LOVE

FAITH - Belief or trust in a person, idea, or thing without hard support.

Secondary:

ALLEGIANCE - Loyalty to a cause or ideal.
FAITH
BELIEF - Trust or confidence.
CREDENCE - Acceptance as true.
CREED - A formal statement of belief.
CONFIDENT - Trust or faith in a person or thing; selfassurance.
FIDELITY - Faithfulness to obligations or duties; truth.

PRIME: FEAR

FEAR - Agitation or dismay in the anticipation of or in the presence of danger. - The opposite of "Love".
Secondary:

ALARM - A warning of danger.
CONSTERNATION - Great agitation or dismay.
DISMAY - To fill with dread.
DREAD - To anticipate with alarm.
FRIGHT - Sudden intense fear.
HORROR - An intense feeling of repugnance and fear.
PANIC - A sudden overpowering terror.
TERROR - Intense, overpowering fear.
TREPIDATION - Dread, apprehension.

PRIME: LOVE

FESTIVE - Merry, joyous.
Secondary:

BLITHE - Carefree and lighthearted.
BOISTEROUS - Loud, noisy and unrestrained.

BOUNCY - Vivacious, spirited, exuberant.
CONVIVIAL - Fond of social pleasures.
EFFERVESCENT - To show high spirits or excitement.
ENLIVENED - To make lively or spirited; animate.
FRIVOLOUS - Inappropriately silly.
GAY - Cheerful and lighthearted; merry.
GLEEFUL - To be jubilant with delight; joy.
FESTIVE
HIGH - Indicating excitement or euphoria.
JAUNTY - Being buoyant or with a self-confident air.
JOLLY - Full of good humor.
JOVIAL - Mirthful.
LIGHTHEARTED - Happy and carefree.
MERRY - Full of high-spirited gaiety.
MIRTH - Gladness and gaiety.
SPIRITED - Marked by animation, vigor.
SUNNY - Cheerful; genial.
VITALIZED - To be endowed with life, vigor or energy.
VIVACIOUS - Lively in temper, conduct or spirit.

PRIME: FEAR

FURIOUS - Ragingly angry.

Secondary:

BILE - Ill tempered; irascible.
CHOLERIC - Easily angered; irritable.
EMBITTERED - Intensely hostile or discontented.
ENRAGED - Infuriated; violent.
EXASPERATED - Provoked to anger; impatient.
FUMING - Showing resentment or anger.
HOT - Angry.
INCENSED - Extremely angry; infuriated.
INFLAMED - Aroused with strong feelings or passion.
INFURIATED - Mad with rage.
IRATE - Extremely angry.

IREFUL - Full of wrath.

MAD - Feeling intense anger or resentment.

OUTRAGED - A fierce anger aroused by injustice or indignity.

SEETHING - Unexpressed violent agitation.

PRIME: LOVE

FLIRTATIOUS - To make coy, romantic or sexual overtures.

Secondary:

COQUETTISH - Trifling with another's affections; flirting.

COY - Flirtatiously shy.

KITTENISH - Joyfully affected playfulness.

PLAYFUL - Full of fun; frolicsome

SEDUCTIVE - To entice or beguile.

SPORTIVE - Playful; amorously active.

G

PRIME: FEAR

GUILT- Remorseful awareness of having done something wrong.

Secondary:

ANGST - Feeling of anxiety; remorse; guilt.

CONTRITE - Repentant; penitent.

COMPUNCTION - A strong uneasiness caused by guilt.

PENITENT - Expressing remorse for one's misdeeds.

REGRET - To feel sorry disappointed or distressed about.

REMORSEFUL - Bitter regret for past deeds.

REPENTANT - Contrition for past conduct or sin.

SELF-REPROACHFUL - Full of excess disapproval of oneself.

SHAMEFUL - A painful emotion caused by strong sense of guilt.

SORRY - Regretful, penitent.

H

PRIME: LOVE

HAPPY- State of joy or pleasure.

Secondary:

AMUSED - Stimulated to laugh or smile; entertained.

BEATIFIC - Exhalted joy or bliss.

BLISSFUL - Extremely happy, ecstatic.

CHEERFUL - In good spirits.

DELIGHTED - State of great pleasure.

DELIRIOUS - Experiencing violent emotion or excitement.

ECSTATIC - State of intense joy or delight; rapture.

ELATED - To be proud or joyful.

ENJOY - Receiving pleasure or satisfaction from.

ENRAPTURED - Filled with delight.

EUPHORIC - A feeling of great happiness or well-being.

EXALTED - Elated with joy.

EXHILARATED - To be joyous and energetic.

FELICITOUS - Agreeable manner or style.

FULFILLED - Satisfied.

GAY - Cheerful, lighthearted.

GLAD - Experiencing, showing or giving joy and pleasure.

GRATEFUL - Deeply appreciative.

JOYOUS - Full of joy; gay.

JUBILANT - Exultantly joyful.

OVERJOYED - Filled with delight.

PLEASED - Given pleasure.

RAPTUROUS - A state of ecstasy.

RAVISHED - Overwhelmed with emotion.

TRANSPORTED - Affected strongly with emotion; stimulated.
THRILLED - Enraptured with delight.

PRIME: FEAR

HATE - Feeling hostility or animosity toward; detest.
Secondary:
ABHOR - To regard with loathing.
ABOMINATE - To detest thoroughly
HATE
ANIMOSITY - Bitter hostility or open enmity.
BITTER - Exhibiting a strong animosity.
CONTEMPT - Disparaging or haughty disdain.
DESPISE - To regard with scorn.
DETEST - To dislike intensely.
DISLIKE - To regard with aversion; distaste.
DISDAINFUL - To treat with contempt.
ENMITY - Deep-seated, often mutual hatred.
EXECRATE - To denounce with loathing.
LOATHE - To dislike greatly.
RANCOROUS - Bitter long lasting resentment.
SCORN - Contempt or disdain.
SPURN - To reject or refuse disdainfully.

PRIME: LOVE

HOPEFUL - Expecting to get what one wants.
Secondary:
ANTICIPATIVE - Feeling expectation.
ASSURED - Confident.
EXPECTANT - Anticipating an event.
SANGUINE - Cheerfully optimistic.

PRIME: FEAR

HUMILIATED - Degraded; lowered in pride, dignity or self-respect of.

Secondary:

ABASED - Humbled.

ABASHED - Ashamed; disconcerted.

ABUSED - Used wrongly or improperly; insulted.

AFFRONTED - Intentionally insulted.

ASHAMED - Affected, embarrassed or disconcerted by shame.

HUMILIATED

BELITTLED - Being thought less of; disparaged.

CHAGRINED - Feeling of embarrassment or annoyance.

CRUSHED - Overwhelmed with humiliation.

DASHED - Depressed; daunted.

DEBASED - Lowered in character.

DEGRADED - To be reduced in status.

DEMEANED -Having one's dignity lowered.

DEPRECIATED - To be diminished in value.

DISCOMFITED - Uneasy or perplexed.

DISESTEEM - Lack of self-confidence.

DISGRACED - Loss of honor.

DISHONORED - Loss of respect, reputation.

DISREPUTED - Disgraced, damaged reputation.

DISPARAGED - To be spoken of in a slighting way.

EMBARRASSED - Caused to be self-conscious or uncomfortable.

GROVELING - Humbling one's self.

HUMBLED - Lowered in rank or station.

IGNOMINY - Personal dishonor.

LOW - Humble or inferior in status.

MORTIFIED - Shamed.

SHAMED - Made to feel guilty through dishonor or disgrace.

I

PRIME: FEAR

IMPASSIONED - Filled with passion; fervent.

Secondary:

ARDOR - Fiery intensity of feeling.
AVID - Having an ardent desire.
BERSERK - Crazed with passion.
FANATICAL - Possessed with extreme zeal.
FERVENT - Greatly emotional or zealous.
IMPASSIONED (Cont.)
FERVID - Extremely passionate.
FRENETIC - Wildly excited or active.
EXCITED - Stimulated with strong emotion; passion.
MAD - Showing strong enthusiasm about something.
MONOMANIACAL - Exaggerated zeal in single thing.
OBSESSED - Preoccupied excessively about something.
PASSION - Boundless enthusiasm; powerful emotion.
ZEAL - Enthusiastic devotion to a cause or goal.

J

PRIME: FEAR

JEALOUS - Resentment or bitterness.

Secondary:

COVETOUS - Excessively desirous of another's possessions.

ENVIOUS - Resentment aroused by desire of another's possessions or qualities.

K

PRIME: LOVE

KINDLY - Of a sympathetic, helpful or benevolent nature.

Secondary:

AFFABLE - Easy and pleasant to speak to.
AMIABLE - Friendly, good natured.
AMITY - Peaceful relations.
BENIGNANT - Kind and gracious.
BENEVOLENT - Performing kind or charitable acts.
CLEMENT - Lenient or merciful.
COMPASSIONATE - Showing deep awareness of suffering of others.
CONGENIAL - Friendly and sociable.
CORDIAL - Warm and sincere.
KINDLY (Continued)
FRIENDLY - Favorably disposed to others.
GRACIOUS - marked by kindness and warm courtesy.
HEARTFELT - Deeply and sincerely earnest.
HEARTY - Expressed warmly and exuberantly.
HOSPITABLE - Cordial and generous.
HUMANE - Kind or compassionate.
SOCIAL - Seeking out and enjoying the company of others.

L

PRIME: FEAR

LASCIVIOUS - Lustful, lecherous; salacious.

Secondary:

CONCUPISCENCE - Sexual desire; lust.
CYPRIANIC - A lewd person; prostitute.
DEBAUCHED - Corrupted morally.
EROTIC - Tending to arouse sexual desire.
GOATISH - Displaying a lecherous demeanor.
LECHEROUS - A person given to lewd or lascivious behavior.
LEWD - Lustful; obscene; indecent.
LIBERTINE - A licentious person.

LIBIDINOUS - Full of lust or lewdness; unrestrained libido.

LICENTIOUS - lacking moral or sexual restraint.

LUBRICIOUS - Lewd; wanton; salacious.

LUSTFUL - Intense, or unrestrained sexual desire.

NYMPHOMANIA - Woman exhibiting abnormally strong and uncontrollable sexual desire.

PRURIENT - Arousing extreme sexual desire.

RANDY - Lecherous.

RUTTISH - Displaying lustful or lascivious behavior or thoughts.

LASCIVIOUS (Continued)

SALACIOUS - Prurient; lascivious.

SATYR LIKE - A lecher.

SENSUAL - Gratification of physical appetites; sexuality.

SEXUAL - Implying erotic desires or activity.

VENERY - The practice of sexual pleasures, sexual indulgence.

WANTON - Immoral or unchaste.

WICKED - Evil by nature and in practice.

PRIME: LOVE

LIKE - Attracted to or pleased by.

Secondary:

AFFINITY - Natural attraction or feeling of kinship.

ATTACHMENT - Bond of affection or loyalty.

ATTRACTED - Interest or admiration.

CARE FOR - Concern or interest.

FAVOR - A liking or preference for.

FANCY - A capricious liking or inclination; drawn to.

FOND - Strong inclination or affection.

INCLINED - Favorably disposed toward.

PARTIAL - Particularly fond.

PREDILECTION - Disposition in favor of something.

PREFER - To choose as more desirable.
REGARD - To hold in esteem or affection.

PRIME: LOVE

LOVE - Is a word of wide range and of varying degrees of intensity. You are pretty much on your own with this one.
Secondary:

ADORE - Deep rapturous love.
AFFECTION - Warm feeling for someone or something.
AMOROUS - Disposed to love, especially sexual love.
BELOVED - Dearly loved.
CHERISH - To hold dear.
CRUSH - Temporary infatuation.
DOTING - Showing excessive love or fondness.
ENAMORED - To inspire with love; captivate.
INFATUATION - Unreasoning love or attachment.
LOVESOME - State of feeling loving or amorous.
NARCISSISTIC - Love of one's self.
PLATONIC - Transcending physical desire.

PRIME: FEAR

LONELY - Without companions; solitary.
Secondary:

ABANDONED - Deserted; forsaken.
ALONE - Apart from others.
DESOLATE - Left alone; forlorn.
DESERTED - To be left alone.
FORLORN - Deserted or abandoned.
FRIENDLESS - To be without a friend.
LONESOME - Sad at feeling alone.
REJECTED - Discarded as useless.
SECLUDED - To be set apart from others.
SEQUESTERED - To segregate into seclusion.
SOLITARY - Existing or living alone.

M

PRIME: FEAR

MISCHIEVOUS - Playful in a naughty or teasing way; pranks.

Secondary:

BLACKGUARDLY - Behaving without principles; scurrilous.

DASTARDLY - Cowardly and sneaky; malicious.

MISCHIEVOUS (Continued)

DEVILISH - Excessively fiendish.

IMPISH - Child of the Devil.

KNAVISH - Unprincipled and crafty.

MALICIOUS - Desiring to harm others or see them suffer.

NAUGHTY - Disobediently mischievous; badly behaved.

PRANKISH - Mischievous trickery; joker.

PUCKISH - Mischievous in a childlike way; impish.

ROGUISH - Unprincipled scoundrel.

SCOUNDRELLY - Villainous behavior.

SLY - Playfully underhanded or deceitful.

VILLAINOUS - Evil scoundrel.

WICKED - Playfully mischievous.

PRIME: FEAR

MOURNFUL - Expressing grief or lamentation.

Secondary:

AFFLICTED - Beset by feelings of distress and grief.

BALEFUL - Full of woe, sorrow.

BLACK - Depressed, gloomy.

DIRGEFUL - Mournful as in a funeral song.

DOLEFUL - Filled with grief.

DOLOROUS - Filled with sorrow; sadness.

DREARY - To be dismal or gloomy.

FUNEREAL - Suggestive of a funeral.

HEARTBROKEN - Suffering overwhelming sorrow.

LUGUBRIOUS - Mournful or gloomy to a ludicrous degree.

MELANCHOLY - Sad, depressed.

SOLEMN - Gloomy; somber.

SOMBER - Gloomy; melancholy.

SORROWFUL - Full of mental distress caused by suffering.

WISTFUL - Pensively sad; melancholy.

WEEPY - A weeping or mournful state.

MOURNFUL (Cont.)

WOEFUL - Afflicted by distress or misfortune.

MOODY - Given to changeable temperament.

BROODING - Thinking deeply; worrying.

MERCURIAL - Quick and changeable in temperament.

MOROSE - Sullenly melancholy.

SATURNINE - Morose and sardonic.

SHORT-TEMPERED - Easily moved to anger.

SOMBER - Dismal; melancholy.

SULK - Aloof or withdrawn.

SULLEN - Gloomy or somber.

VOLATILE - Tending to vary often.

N

PRIME: FEAR

NERVOUS - Agitated; high-strung; jumpy and uneasy.

Secondary:

AGITATED - Excited and disturbed.

ANXIETY - State of apprehension.

ANXIOUS - Uneasy and apprehensive.

CONCERNED - Interested; anxious and troubled.

EDGY - Irritable; anxious.

DISQUIETUDE - A condition of worried unease; anxiety.

DISTRAUGHT - Deeply agitated or anxious.

FIDGETY - Restless; jumpy.
FRANTIC - Distraught from fear or worry.
FRAZZLED - Emotionally exhausted.
FRETFUL - Irritated; annoyed.
HYSTERICAL - Uncontrollable outburst of emotion.
JUMPY - On edge.
OVERWROUGHT - Extremely nervous and agitated.
PANICKY - Afflicted with sudden overpowering terror.
RAVING - Behaving irrationally.

NERVOUS (Cont.)

RESTLESS - Not able to relax or be still.
SENSITIVE - Easily irritated, aware.
STRAINED - Showing signs of nervous tension.
STRESSED - In a state of extreme nervous difficulty.
TENSE - Nervous tension; tightness.
UNEASY - Lacking sense of security.
UNSETTLED - Disordered or disturbed.
WORRIED - Feeling uneasy or troubled; anxious.

O

PRIME: FEAR

OPPRESSED - Weighed down heavily in mind or spirit; burdened.

Secondary:

BURDENED - Bearing something emotionally difficult.
ENCUMBERED - To be weighed down.
ENSLAVED - Subject or dominated by.
DOWNTRODDEN - Oppressed, tyrannized.
OBSEQUIOUS - Full of servile compliance.
PRAYED UPON - Made victim of.
PRESSED - Influenced by insistent argument.
SERVILE - Abjectly submissive.
SUBDUED - To subjugate; vanquish.
SUBJUGATED - Under control; conquered; subservient.

SUBSERVIENT - Servile.
SUPPRESSED - Inhibited from expression.
TAXED - To make heavy demands on.
TYRANNIZED - Subjected to excessive or cruel behavior; ruled.

PRIME: FEAR
OVERWHELMED - To be defeated completely.
Secondary:
BEATEN - Conquered; defeated; baffled; dejected.
CONQUERED - Defeated or subdued as in by force.
DEFEATED - Overcome; beaten.
DEVASTATED - Lay wasted.
ROUTED - Driven or forced out; beaten.
OVERCOME - Defeated; conquered.
VANQUISHED - Overcome; subdued; beaten.

P

PRIME: FEAR
PESSIMISTIC - Taking the gloomiest possible view of a situation.
Secondary:
CYNICAL - Sneering at the sincerity of motives.
DESPAIRING - Belittling.
GLOOMY - Dark and depressing.
HOPELESS - Feeling no hope.
MISANTHROPIC - The feeling of hating mankind.
MISOGYNOUS - Hatred of women.

PRIME: FEAR
PROUD - Feeling self-respect, worth or esteem.
Secondary:
ARROGANT - Unpleasantly or disdainfully self-important.
COCKY - Overly self-confident.

CONCEITED - Vain, self importance; self-centered..
DIGNIFIED - A state of being worthy of respect; noble.
ELATED - Proud or joyful; full of delight.
HAUGHTY - Condescendingly proud.
HONORED - Held in high esteem.
NSOLENT - Disrespectfully arrogant.
PROUD (Cont.)
LOFTY - Exhalted; noble.
OSTENTATIOUS - Extravagantly showy; pretentious.
PRETENTIOUS - Claiming merit, especially when not justified.
POMPOUS - Self-important.
SELF-ESTEEMED - Confident; self-respect.
VAIN - Excessively proud or conceited.

Q

PRIME: FEAR

QUARRELSOME - Given to quarreling; contentious.

Secondary:

ARGUMENTATIVE - Given to argue; disputatious.
BILIOUS - Irascible.
CANTANKEROUS - Ill-tempered and quarrelsome.
CHURLISH - Rude, surly person.
CONTENTIOUS - Argumentative.
CRABBY - Grouchy; ill tempered.
CRANKY - Ill-tempered.
CROTCHETY - Peevish.
DISPUTATIOUS - Inclined to dispute.
FRACTIOUS - Having a cranky nature; peevish.
GRUMPY - Cranky and complaining.
HUFFY - Quick to take offense.
IRASCIBLE - Easily angered.
LIVERISH - Acting bilious; peevish.

PETULANT - Unreasonably irritable or ill-tempered.
PEEVISH - Querulous or discontented.
QUERULOUS - Given to complaining.
SPLENETIC - Ill-humored; irritable.
TESTY - Irritable; touchy.

R

PRIME: FEAR

RAPACIOUS - Greedy, ravenous.

Secondary:

ACQUISITIVE - Eager to gain and possess.
AVARICIOUS - Extreme desire for wealth; greed.
AVID - Having an ardent desire or craving.
DESIROUS - Wanting, desiring.
DEMANDING - Requiring much effort or attention.
GREEDY - Wanting to possess more than one needs or deserves.
VORACIOUS - Enormous appetite for something.

S

PRIME: FEAR

SAD - Sorrowful; unhappy; melancholy.

Secondary:

CHEERLESS - Low in spirits.
DEJECTED - Depressed; low in spirits.
DEPRESSED - Low in spirits; dejected; blue.
DESPONDENT - Loss of hope.
DESOLATE - Forlorn.
DISCONSOLATE - Hopelessly sad.
DISMAL - Causing or showing gloom or depression.
DOLEFUL - Filled with grief.
DOLOROUS - Filled with sorrow.
HEAVY-HEARTED - Melancholy; depressed; sad.
LUGUBRIOUS - Mournful, to a ludicrous degree.

MELANCHOLY - Habitual sadness or depression.
MISERABLE - Very unhappy; wretched.
MOROSE - Sullenly melancholy.
WRETCHED - Woeful; miserable.
WOEFUL - Distressed from grief.

PRIME: LOVE

SENTIMENTAL - Characterized or swayed by sentiment or emotions.

Secondary:

DREAMY - Given to dreams or fantasy.
EMOTIONAL - Readily affected with emotion.
EMPATHETIC - Understanding another's feelings and motives.
FANCIFUL - Marked by fancy or unrestrained imagination.
GUSHY - Over effusive.
MAUDLIN - Tearfully sentimental.
MAWKISH - Excessively and objectionably sentimental.
MUSHY - Marked my maudlin sentimentality.
ROMANTIC - Given to thoughts or feelings of romance or love.

PRIME: LOVE

SERENE - Tranquil; calm and unruffled.

Secondary:

BLITHE - Carefree and lighthearted.
CALM - Not excited or agitated.
COMFORTED - A condition of pleasurable ease or well-being.
COMPLACENCE - Contented self-satisfaction.
COMPOSED - Serenely self-possessed.
CONTENTED - At ease.
COOL - Marked by calm self-control.

DISPASSIONATE - Not influenced by emotion or bias.
EASE - Freedom from pain, worry or agitation.
MELLOW - Relaxed; easygoing.
PEACEFUL - In harmony with one's self; calm.
PLACID - Undisturbed by tumult or disorder.
SEDATE - Calm and deliberate in character and manner.
TRANQUIL - Free from agitation; calm.

PRIME: FEAR

SHOCKED - A violent, unexpected disturbance of mental or emotional balance.

Secondary:

AGAPE - With the mouth wide open, as in wonder.
AGHAST - Struck by terror or amazement.
AMAZED - Full of great wonder.
APPALLED - Filled with horror or dismay.
ASTONISHED - Filled with sudden wonder or amazement.
ASTOUNDED - Astonished and bewilder.
CONSTERNATED - Greatly agitated or dismayed.
STARTLED - Alarmed or surprised suddenly.
STUPEFIED - Overwhelmed with amazement or shock.
SURPRISED - Amazement from something unexpected.
THUNDERSTRUCK - Astonished; stunned.

T

PRIME: FEAR

TIMID - Shy; fearful and hesitant.

Secondary:

BASHFUL - Shy and self-conscious
COWARDLY - Lacking courage.
DIFFIDENT- Lacking self confidence.
DEMURE - Modest in manner.
DOCILE - Tractable.

INHIBITED - Restrained.
INSECURE - Lacking self-confidence.
MEEK - Submissive; passive.
MODEST - Retiring; shy.
PUSILLANIMOUS - Lacking courage; cowardly.
SHEEPISH - Excessively submissive.
SHY - Drawing back from contact with others; reserved.
SUBMISSIVE - Humble; obedient.
UNAGRESSIVE - Retiring.
UNOSTENTATIOUS - Discreet.
UNPRETENTIOUS - Modest.

PRIME: FEAR

TRUCULENT - Disposed to fight; pugnacious.

Secondary:

BELLIGERENT - Eager to fight; hostile.
EMBITTERED - To arouse bitter feelings in.
ENVENOMED - Embittered.
FEROCIOUS - Extremely savage.
FIERCE - Having a violent nature.
PUGNACIOUS - Combative in nature; belligerent.
SAVAGE - Ferocious; fierce.
WRATHFUL - Furious, often vindictive anger.

U

PRIME: FEAR

UNFEELING - Not sympathetic; callous; insentient.

Secondary:

ALOOF - Distant or reserved in manner; apart.
AUSTERE - Stern, solemn; disciplined.
CALLOUS - Insensitive; indifferent.
COLD-HEARTED - (Hard-hearted) Lacking sympathy or feelings.
FRIGID - Lacking warmth of feeling.

GRUDGING - Feeling of resentment.
HEARTLESS - Devoid of compassion.
IMPASSIVE - Revealing no emotion; expressionless.
INSENSITIVE - Unaffected by the feelings of others.
INSENTIENT -Devoid of sensation.
NIGGARDLY - Grudging and petty; stingy.
NUMB - Stunned, as from shock.
UNFEELING (Cont.)
RESERVED - Marked by self-restraint and reticence.
RIGID - Stiff or fixed in feelings.
UNEMOTIONAL - Feeling no emotion at all; impassive.
UNMOVED - Unaffected by emotion.

V

PRIME: LOVE

VALIANT - Possessing, showing or acting with valor; brave.

Secondary:

ADVENTUROUS - Undertaking new and daring enterprises.

AUDACIOUS - Fearlessly daring.

BRAVE - Possessing or displaying courage.

BRAZEN - Facing with bold self-assurance.

BOLD - Daring; exhibiting courage and bravery.

CHIVALROUS - Qualities such as bravery, honor and gallantry.

COURAGE - Quality of mind enabling one to face danger; bravery.

DARING - Bold and venturesome.

DOUGHTY - Stouthearted and brave.

FEARLESS - To be without fear.

GALLANT - Nobly courageous.

HEROIC - Nobly or selflessly brave.

INTREPID - Resolutely courageous.

NERVY - Bold, daring.
PROWESS - Superior strength and courage.
STOUTHEARTED - Brave; courageous.
UNDAUNTED - Resolutely courageous.
VALOR - Courage and boldness as in battle.

W

PRIME: LOVE

WARMHEARTED - Kind; friendly and compassionate.

Secondary:

AFFECTIONATE - Tender and warm feeling toward another.
AFFINITY - A natural attraction or feeling of kinship.
CARING - Feeling and exhibiting concern and empathy.
GOODHEARTED - Kind and generous.
SOFTHEARTED - Easily moved.
TENDER - Gentle and loving.
WARM - Friendly; kindly affectionate.

X

PRIME: FEAR

XENOPHOBIC - Unduly fearful or contemptuous of strangers or foreigners.

Secondary:

CONSECRATE - To declare or set apart as sacred.
PATRIOTIC - Devoted to the well-being of one's country.

Y

PRIME: FEAR

YEARN - To have a strong or deep desire.

Secondary:

COVET - to desire that which is rightfully another's.
CRAVE - To want intensely.
DESIRE - To wish or long for; want.

FAMISHED - Suffering for lack of something necessary.
HANKER - A strong, often restless desire.
HUNGER - A strong desire or craving.
LONG - An earnest desire.
PINING - Yearning intensely for something unattainable.
YEARN (Cont.)
WANT - To desire or wish for.
WISH - A desire or longing for something.
YEN - Yearning or craving.

Z

PRIME: LOVE

ZEALOUS - Fervent; full of or motivated by zeal.

Secondary:

ARDENT - Characterized by passion.
AMBITIOUS - Full of or motivated by ambition.
DEVOTED - Feeling strong attachment.
EAGER - Showing keen interest.
EARNEST - Showing deep sincerity or seriousness.
EBULLIENT - Zestfully enthusiastic.
ENTHUSIASTIC - Great excitement in a subject or cause.
EXUBERANT - High-spirited; lively.
FERVENT - Greatly emotional or zealous.
FERVID - Passionate.
GUNG HO - Extremely enthusiastic and dedicated.
ZEALOUS (Cont.)
KEEN - Ardent; enthusiastic.
PASSIONATE - Affected by strong emotion.
TRENCHANT - Keen; incisive.
VERVE - Enthusiasm, vitality.
ZEAL - Enthusiastic devotion to a cause or ideal.

"It is just as hard to make a toilet seat as a castle window.
But the view is different."
- Ben Hecht -

PHOTOS

LONE STAR
From
the
Big Country

ADMIT
ONE

ROCKABILLY BABY

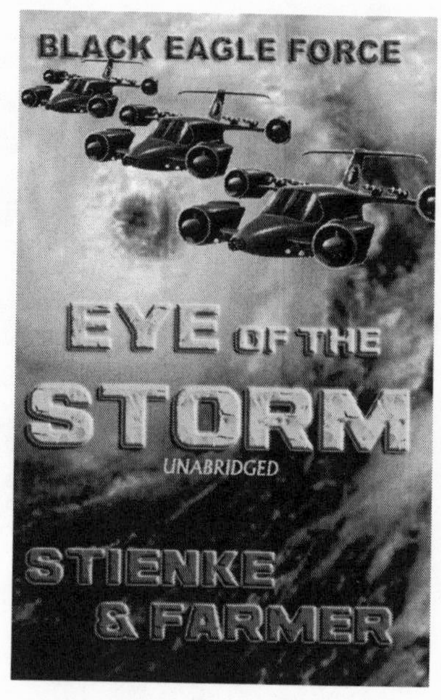

BUCK STIENKE

M600A BLACK EAGLE

BLACK EAGLE FORCE
BUCK STIENKE
KEN FARMER

A BLACK EAGLE FORCE NOVEL
Buck STIENKE
FARMER
Return of the
STARFIGHTER

THE
NATIONS
CHEROKEE
CREEK
SEMINOLE
CHICKASAW
CHOCTAW
DEPUTY MARSHAL
I.T.
UNITED
STATES
4
Not just a thrilling saga of the American west
...it is a triumph! - Dwight Jon Zimmerman
KEN FARMER
BUCK STIENKE

GLOSSARY
of
TERMS

CRAFT TERMINOLOGY GLOSSARY

ABBY SINGER - The shot before the last shot of the day. Named in honor of former first A.D., Abby Singer, who used to call the last shot of the day one shot too early.

ACTION - The command from the director for the scene to begin. It indicates that the camera is rolling.

A.D.- The Assistant Director.

AD LIB - Extemporaneous delivery without relying on a prepared script.

ADR - Automated Dialogue Replacement or Additional Dialogue Recording. Dialogue added to a scene in post production. Sometimes erroneously called "looping".

AEA - Actors' Equity Association; often called simply "Equity". SAG's sister union which represents stage actors and stage managers.

AFI - The American Film Institute

AFTRA - American Federation of Television and Radio Artists. Represents radio artists and news broadcasters, and, in earlier times, television performers. In more recent times, however, television performers may be represented by either AFTRA or SAG, depending on the producer's contract. Discussions about merging the two organizations have been ongoing for several decades; recent Television & Film and Commercial Contracts have been jointly negotiated.

AGMA - American Guild of Musical Artists

AGVA - American Guild of Variety Artists

ART DIRECTOR - Person who conceives and designs the sets.

AUDITION - A tryout for a film, TV or stage role. Usually auditions involving reading from the script, but can also require improvisation.

AVAIL - A courtesy situation extended by performer or agent to a producer indicating availability to work a certain job. Avails have no legal or contractual status.

BACKGROUND - The Extra performers. On the set, "Background!" is a verbal cue for the Extras to start their action.

BACK TO ONE - The verbal cue for performers to return to the mark where they started the scene.

BEAUTY SHOT - On TV soaps, the shot over which the credits are rolled.

BEST BOY - The assistant to the Chief Electrician, or Head Gaffer.

BILLING - The order of the names in the title of opening credits of a film or TV show.

BIO - Short for "biography". A resume in narrative form, usually for a printed program or press release.

BLOCKING - The actual physical movements by performers in any scene. Also can refer to the movements of the camera.

BOOKING - A firm commitment to a performer to do a specific job.

BOOM - An overhead microphone, usually on an extended pole. The Boom Operator is the member of the sound department responsible for holding the boom pole, with mic attached, over and sometimes under the actors. Also usually responsible for placing radio mics on actors.

BLUE SCREEN/GREEN SCREEN - Shooting in a studio against a large blue or greenish backdrop, which allows a background to be superimposed later on the final image. The actors must imagine the set they are on and be aware of the limitations of their movements.

BREAKAWAY - Specially designed prop or set piece which looks solid but shatters easily. Breakaways props are often glass items.
BREAKDOWN - A detailed listing and description of roles available for casting in a production.

CALLBACK - Any follow-up interview or audition.

CALL SHEET - A sheet containing the cast and crew call times for a specific day's shooting. Scene numbers, the expected day's total pages, locations, and production needs and props are also included.

CALL TIME - The actual time an actor is due on the set.

CAMERA CREW - With the D.P. (Director of Photography) as its chief, this team consists of the camera operator, the first assistant camera operator (focus puller), the second assistant camera operator (film loader and clapstick clapper) and the dolly grip.

CAMERA OPERATOR - The member of the camera crew who actually looks through the lens during a take. Responsible for panning and tilting and keeping the action within the frame.

CAMERA LEFT/RIGHT - Means left/right from the camera's point of view.

CASTING DIRECTOR - The producer's representative responsible for screening performers for consideration by the producer or director.

CATTLE CALL - A call for large groups of people.

CATERER - Responsible for breakfast, lunch and dinner on a set. Different from Craft Services.

CD-ROM - A compact disk that holds text, music and images. One of the principal new venues for interactive video games as well as for full motion video films. Acting for CD-ROM's is a new arena for actors. SAG 's Interactive Media Contract covers salaries and working conditions for this new medium.

CG - Computer Generated.

CHANGES - Outfits worn while performing.

CHEAT - The actor's adjustment of body position away from what might be absolutely "natural" in order to accommodate the camera; can also mean looking in a different place from where the other actor actually is.

CHECKING THE GATE! - A verbal command to check the lens on the camera; if the lens is - OK - the cast & crew will move on to the next scene or shot.

CHIEF ELECTRICIAN - Heads the electrician crew; also called the Gaffer.

CINEMATOGRAPHER - Director of Photography

CLOSE-UP (CU) - Camera term for tight shot of shoulders and face.

COLD READING - Unrehearsed reading of a scene, usually at an audition.

COMMISSION - Percentage of a performer's earnings paid to agents or managers for services rendered.

COMPOSITE - A series of photos on one sheet representing an actor's different looks.

CONFLICT - Status of being paid for services in a commercial for one advertiser, thereby contractually preventing performing services in a commercial for a competitor.

COPY - The script for a commercial or voice over.

COVERAGE - All camera shots other than the master shot; coverage might include two-shots and close-ups.

CRAFT SERVICES - Onset beverage and snack table. Different from the Caterer

CRANE SHOT - A camera shot raised over or above the set or the action.

CRAWL - Usually the end credits in a film or TV shot which "crawl" up the screen.

CREDITS - Opening or closing names in a film or TV show; also refers to a one's performance experience listed on a resume or in a program
CU - Close up shot.

CUE - Signal, often an off-stage light or hand signal, by the assistant director to indicate an actor's entrance or action.

CUT! - The verbal cue for the action of the scene to stop. At no time, may an actor call, "cut!"

CUTAWAY - A short scene between two shots of the same person, showing something other than that person.

DAILIES - Screening of footage before it is edited.

DAY PLAYER (DAY PERFORMER) - A principal performer hired on a daily basis, rather than on a longer-term contract.

DAYTIME DRAMA - Soap opera.

DEMO TAPE - An audio or video tape that agents use for audition purposes

DGA - Directors Guild of America.

DIALECT - A distinctly regional or linguistic speech pattern.

DIALOGUE - The scripted words exchanged by performers.

DIRECTOR - The coordinator of all artistic and technical aspects of any production.

DIRECTOR OF PHOTOGRAPHY (D.P. or Cinematographer) - Supervises all decisions regarding lighting, camera lenses, color and filters, camera angle set-ups, camera crew and film processing.

DOLLY - A piece of equipment that the camera sits on to allow mobility of the camera.

DOLLY GRIP - The crew member who moves the dolly.

DOUBLE - A performer who appears in place of another performer, i.e., as in a stunt or body double.

D.P. - Director of Photography or Cinematographer.

DRESS THE SET - Add such items to the set as curtains, furniture, props, etc.

DRIVE-ON PASS - In Los Angeles, a pass to drive onto and park on a studio lot.

DUPE - A duplicate copy of a film or tape; also, a "dub"

8x10 - Commonly used size of a performer's photos, usually in black and white.

18-TO-PLAY-YOUNGER - A performer legally 18 years old, who can convincingly be cast as a younger age.

ECU - Extreme close-up.

ELECTRICIAN - In film, crew members who place lighting instruments, focus, gel and maneuver the lights.

EMPLOYER OF RECORD (EOR) - The company responsible for employment taxes, unemployment benefits and workers compensation coverage.
EQUITY - Actors Equity Association (AEA) Union representing stage actors.

EQUITY WAIVER - In Los Angeles, 99-seat (or less) theatres which were otherwise professional, over which Equity waived contract provisions under certain circumstances. Now officially called "Showcase code", the term "Equity waiver" is still used informally.

EXECUTIVE PRODUCER - Person responsible for funding the production.

EXT. (Exterior) - A scene shot outside.

EXTRA - Background talent, used only in non-principal roles.

FICA - Social Security taxes (Federal Insurance Corporation of America).
FIELD REP. - Union staff member who ensures contractual compliance on sets.

FIRST A.D. - First Assistant Director; person responsible for the running of the set. Gives instructions to crew and talent, including calling for "first team," "quiet," "rehearsal," and "take five", ect.

FIRST ASSISTANT CAMERA OP. - First Assistant Camera Operator is responsible for focusing the camera lens during the shooting of a scene; also known as the Focus Puller.

FIRST TEAM - The production term for the principal actors in a scene.

4-A's - Associated Actors and Artists of America; umbrella organization for SAG, AFTRA, Equity and other performers' Unions.

FORCED CALL - A call to work less than 12 hours after dismissal on the previous day. See TURNAROUND.

FOREGROUND CROSS - Action in a scene in which an Extra Performer passes between the camera and the principal actors; sometimes called a "wipe".

FX (Effects) - Special Effects.

GAFFER - The Chief Electrician.

GOLDEN TIME - Contractually called 16 Hour Rule Violation for Extra Performers, is overtime, after the 16th hour, paid in units of one full day per hour.

GRIPS - Members of the film crew who are responsible for moving set pieces, lighting equipment, dolly track and other physical movement of equipment.

HAND MODEL - A performer whose hands are used to double for others.

HIATUS - Time during which a TV series is not in production

HOLDING - The designated area to which the Extra Performers report and stay while waiting to go on set.
HONEY WAGON - A towed vehicle containing one or more dressing rooms, as well as crew bathrooms.

IATSE - International Alliance of Theatrical Stage Employees; the union which represents most off-camera crew members.
INDUSTRIAL - Non-broadcast film or video, usually of an educational or safety nature

INSERTS - Shots, usually close-ups of hands or close business, inserted into previously shot footage.

INT. (Interior) - A scene shot indoors.

"IN" TIME - The actual call time or start time; also, return time from a break.

LINE PRODUCER - The producer responsible for keeping the director on time and budget; generally the most visible producer actually on the set.

LONG SHOT (LS) - A camera shot which captures the performer's full body.

LOOPING - An in-studio technique used to fix dialogue already performed during principal photography by matching voice to picture.

MARK - The exact position(s) given to an actor on a set to insure that he/she is in the proper light and camera angle; generally marked on the ground with tape or chalk.

MARKER - A verbal cue that the take has been identified on camera both verbally and with the slate board.

MARTINI SHOT - The last shot of the day.

MASTER SHOT - A camera shot that includes the principal actors and relevant background activity; generally used as a reference shot to record the scene from beginning to end before shooting close-ups, over-the-shoulders, etc.
MATCHING ACTIONS - The requirement that the actor match the same physical movements in a scene from take to take in order to preserve the visual continuity.

MEAL PENALTY - A fee paid by the producer for the failure to provide meals or meal breaks as specified by the contract.

MIXER - Chief of the sound crew; responsible for the quality of the sound recording on a shoot.

MOS (Mit Out Sound/Motion Only Shot) - Any shot without dialogue or sound recording. (There's a story behind this)

M.O.W. - Movie of the week.

MS - Medium shot.

MULTIPLE CAMERA - The use of more than one camera for a set up. Camera “A”, “B” and “C”, ect.

ND MEAL (NON DEDUCTIBLE MEAL) - A 15 minute meal break provided to actors by the production company to bring actors in sync with crew break time. It must be completed within 2 hours of performers call time.

NIGHT PREMIUM - A surcharge for certain work performed after 8 p.m.

OFF-CAMERA (OC or OS) - Dialogue delivered without being on screen.

OUT OF FRAME - An actor outside the camera range.

"OUT" TIME - The actual time when you are released after you have changed out of wardrobe and make-up.

OVER-THE-SHOULDER - A shot over the shoulder of one actor, focusing entirely on the face and upper torso of the other actor in a scene; generally shot in pairs so both actors expressions can later be edited together.

OVERDUBBING - In studio singing or voice work, the process of laying one soundtrack over another.

OVERTIME (OT) - Work extending beyond the contractual work day.

P.A. - Production Assistant.

PAN - A camera shot which sweeps from side-to-side.

PAYMASTER - An independent talent payment service acting as the employer of record.

PENSION & HEALTH PAYMENT - An additional amount of money paid by the employer to cover employee benefits under union contract

PER DIEM - Fee paid by producer on location shoots to compensate performer for expenditures for meals not provided by the producer.

PHOTO DOUBLE - An actor cast to perform on camera in place of another.

PICK UP - Starting a scene from a place other than the beginning.

PICK-UP SHOT – Reshooting a portion of a scene, the rest of which was acceptably filmed in a previous take.

PICTURE'S UP - Warning that the sequence of cues to shoot a scene is about to begin.

POV SHOT - Point-of-View shot; camera angle from the perspective of one actor.

POST-PRODUCTION - The phase of filmmaking that begins after the film has been shot. Includes scoring, sound and picture editing, titling, dubbing, and releasing.

PRE-PRODUCTION - The phase of filmmaking before shooting begins; includes writing, scouting locations, budgeting, casting, hiring crews, ordering equipment and creating a shooting schedule.

PRINCIPAL - A performer with lines.

"PRINT" - A call from the director at the end of a take that that particular take is good enough be printed.

PRODUCER - Often called the Line Producer or Show Runner; the person responsible for the day-to-day decision-making on a production.

PRODUCTION COMPANY - The company actually making the film or television show.

PROPS - Any objects used by actors in a scene.

PSA - Public Service Announcement.

REACTION SHOT – A shot of a player listening while another player's voice continues on the sound track.

RESIDUAL - The fee paid to a performers for rebroadcast of a commercial, film or TV program

RESUME - List of credits, usually attached to an 8x10 or composite.

REWRITE - Changes in the script, often using color-coded pages to indicate most current version.

RIGHT-TO-WORK-STATES - Those states where you don't have to be a member of a union to work.

ROLL CAMERA - The verbal cue for the camera film and audio tape to start rolling.

ROLLING - The verbal confirmation from the camera operator that the camera is rolling.

ROOM TONE - A sound recording (sometimes made upon completion of a scene) to record existing noise at the location. Also called "wild track" or "ambient track".

SAG - Screen Actors Guild.

SCALE - Minimum payment for services under union contracts.

SCRIPT - The written form of a screenplay, teleplay, radio or stage play.

SCRIPT SUPERVISOR - The crew member assigned to record all changes or actions as the production proceeds.

SDI - State Disability Insurance.

SECOND ASSISTANT DIRECTOR - Often two or three on a set, they handle checking in the talent, insuring proper paperwork is filed, distribute script revisions. Actors check in with the 2nd A.D. upon arrival on the set.

SECOND TEAM - The verbal cue for the stand-ins to come to the set and be ready to stand in.

SEGUE - In film or tape editing, a transition from one shot to another.

SET - The immediate location where the scene is being filmed.

SET-UP - Each time the camera changes position.

SFX - Sound effects.

SIDES - Pages or scenes from a script, used in auditions or (if on a film set) those scenes being shot that day.

SIGNATORY - An employer who has agreed to produce under the terms of a union contract.

SLATE - A small chalkboard and clapper device, often electronic, used to mark and identify shots on film for editing; also the process of verbal identification by a performer in a taped audition (e.g., "Slate your name!").

SPEED! - A verbal cue that the audio tape is up to speed for recording.

SPIKING THE LENS - Looking directly into the lens during a scene; since it destroys the illusion of realism, actors should never spike the lens unless specifically directed to do so for specific effect.

STAGE RIGHT- To the performer's right side, to the audience's left side. Likewise, STAGE LEFT is to the performer's left, the audience's right. Stage directions are for actors, not audiences, therefore they are always given from the actor's point of view to the audience.

STANDARD UNION CONTRACT - The standard format/contract approved by the Unions and offered to performers prior to the job.

STANDARDS & PRACTICES - The network TV censorship departments.

STAND-INS - Extra Performers used as substitutes for featured players, for the purpose of setting lights and rehearsing camera moves; also known as the second team.

"STICKS" - Slate or clapboard.

STUDIO - A building, recording room or sound stage which accommodates film or TV production.

STUNT COORDINATOR - The person in charge of designing and supervising the performance of stunts and hazardous activities.

STUNT DOUBLE - A stuntperson who performs stunts for a principal.

STUNTPERSON - A specially trained performer who actually performs stunts.

SUBMISSION - An agent's suggestion to a casting director for a role in a certain production.

SUPER - Super impose or to lay one scene over the other.

SW - A notation on a call sheet that an actor is starting on that day and working on that day.

SWF - A notation on a call sheet that an actor is starting, working, and finished on that day.

SWEETENING - In singing/recording, the process of adding additional voices to previously recorded work.

SYNDICATION - Selling TV programs to individual stations rather than to networks.

TAFT-HARTLEY - A federal statute which allows 30 days after first employment before being required to join a Union.

TAKE - The clapboard indication of a shot "taken" or printed.

TAKE 5 - The announcement of periodic five minute breaks.

TELEPROMPTER - The brand name of a device which enables a broadcaster to read a script while looking into the camera lens.

THEATRICAL - TV shows or feature film work, as opposed to commercials.

THREE BELLS - An audible warning for QUIET because a scene is about to be filmed.

TIGHT SHOT (Go in Tight) - Framing of a shot with little or no space around the central figure(s) of feature(s); usually a close-up.

TILT - The up and down movement of a camera.
TIME-AND-A-HALF - Overtime payment of 1 1/2 times the hourly rate.

TRACKING SHOT - A shot taken while the camera is moving, either on a dolly or a mounted on a moving vehicle.

TRADES - Short for "trade papers" - The newspapers and periodicals such as the Hollywood Reporter and Variety that specifically feature information on the entertainment industry.

TURNAROUND - (a) The number of hours between dismissal one day and call time the next day. (b) To shoot a scene from another direction.

TWO-SHOT - A camera framing two persons.

UNDERSTUDY - A performer hired to do a role only if the featured player is unable to perform; used primarily in live theatre.

UPGRADE - The promotion of an extra performer in a scene to the category of principal performer.

UPM - Unit Production Manager - Oversees the crews and is handles the scheduling and all the technical responsibilities of the production.

UP STAGE - (a) The area located at the back of the stage. Down Stage is the area in front of the performer. (b) To draw attention to oneself at the expense of a fellow performer.

VIDEO ASSIST - On site video monitor with playback. Most productions, even if it is "Film", will have Video Assist to view the take on the spot.

VO - Voice over. An off-camera voice coming either from an actor not in the frame, or from a secondary source such as a speakerphone or answering machine.

VOUCHER - Time slip with all pertinent information needed for getting paid properly.

W - A notation on the call sheet indicating that an actor is working that day.

WAIVERS - Union-approved permission for deviation from the terms of a contract.

WALKAWAY - A meal break in which all cast and crew are on their own to get lunch.

WALLA WALLA – The "walla walla" sound of many people in a crowded situation, without specific voices or words being distinguishable.

WARDROBE - The clothing a performer wears on camera.

WARDROBE ALLOWANCE - A maintenance fee paid to on-camera talent for the use (and cleaning) of talent's own clothing.

WARDROBE FITTING - A session held prior to production to prepare a performer's costumes.

WEATHER PERMIT CALL - Due to weather conditions, the production company has the option to release an actor four hours after the call time (if the camera has not started to roll) with a reduced rate of pay for the day.

W/N - Will Notify. A notation on a call sheet that tells the actor that he/she will probably work that day but the specific time has not yet been decided.

WRAP - The completion of a day's filming or of an entire production.

ZOOM - A camera technique with a special lens to adjust the depth of a shot, accomplished without moving the camera.

"THAT'S A WRAP!"